Intrinsic Motivation at Work

Intrinsic Motivation at Work

Building Energy & Commitment

KENNETH W. THOMAS

BK

BERRETT-KOEHLER PUBLISHERS, INC.
San Francisco

Berrett-Koehler Publishers, Inc.
450 Sansome Street, Suite 1200
San Francisco, CA 94111-3320
Tel: (415) 288-0260   Fax: (415) 362-2512
www.bkconnection.com

ORDERING INFORMATION

Individual sales. Berrett-Koehler publications are available through most bookstores. They can also be ordered direct from Berrett-Koehler at the address above.

Quantity sales. Special discounts are available on quantity purchases by corporations, associations, and others. For details, contact the "Special Sales Department" at the Berrett-Koehler address above.

Orders for college textbook/course adoption use. Please contact Berrett-Koehler Publishers at the address above.

Orders by U.S. trade bookstores and wholesalers. Please contact Publishers Group West, 1700 Fourth Street, Berkeley, CA 94710. Tel: 510-528-1444; Fax: 510-528-3444.

Printed in the United States of America

Printed on acid-free and recycled paper that is composed of 50% recycled fiber, including 10% postconsumer waste.

Library of Congress Cataloging-in-Publication Data

Thomas, Kenneth Wayne, 1943-
    Intrinsic motivation at work : building energy and commitment / Kenneth W. Thomas.
      p. cm.
    Includes bibliographical references and index.
    ISBN 1-57675-087-6 (alk. paper)
    1. Employee motivation. I. Title.

HF5549.5.M63 T456 2000
658.3'14—dc21

                                       99-059479

First Edition

04 03 02 01 00   10 9 8 7 6 5 4 3 2 1

Book Production: Pleasant Run Publishing Services
Composition: Classic Typography

To Gail and Sarah

Contents

Preface

This book comes from a sixteen-year program of research. But in a very real way, it began for me with a need to better understand my own experience of work. Like most people, I found that my energies for work could rise and fall dramatically. In my years at UCLA in the 1970s, for example, I was mostly doing research on conflict management in organizations. I would have periods of excitement and fulfillment when being very productive was its own reward. I remember being very excited about writing articles that I knew would make a difference. Likewise, I remember the excitement that Ralph Kilmann and I shared when we were putting together our conflict instrument. But there would be other times when I disliked doing the work—when I had to fight myself to get anything done. Meanwhile, I'd be teaching MBA students some prevailing model of motivation based on *economic* reasoning. There was a real disconnect. Those rational-economic models had very little to do with the energy and fulfillment that were so important to my own work.

I began doing research on intrinsic motivation in the 1980s, when it became clear that this same disconnect was becoming a problem for managers. CEOs were trying to "empower" their workers—giving them more autonomy and self-management and trying to energize them to *care passionately* about their work. But the existing models of motivation said little about passion or energy. I was blessed with colleagues who cared as much as I did about these issues. We put together symposiums, conducted studies, did some consulting, and began to get a clearer and clearer understanding of the intrinsic motivation involved in empowerment. My work with Betty Velthouse and Walt Tymon, and later with Erik Jansen, has been picked up by the broader academic literature in management. Those colleagues have now encouraged me to bring our learnings to a larger audience in this book.

As I have written this book, I have tried to balance a number of goals. The first is to give you a solid conceptual framework for understanding intrinsic motivation and why it is vital to the new work. The problem is that most of us have already learned to think about motivation in rational-economic ways, so that kind of thinking seems solid to us, and other ways of thinking often seem "soft." I have tried to give intrinsic motivation that same kind of solidity by laying a firm conceptual foundation in Parts I and II of this book. Part I establishes the need for new models. It discusses the revolution in work, why extrinsic rewards are no longer enough, and the limitations of rational-economic thinking. I have tried to keep this part brief. Then Part II examines the essence of the new work in more detail, emphasizing how purpose has been reintroduced into that work. It discusses how workers are now being asked to self-manage in pursuit of purposes, and then lays out the key steps involved in self-management. Part III, the heart of the book, discusses the four intrinsic rewards that come from—and energize—those self-management steps: a sense of meaningfulness, choice, competence, and progress.

My second goal was to make the book as useful as possible. Frankly, I don't find lists of recommendations very useful. "Here are twenty things you can try" makes me yawn—not rush out and start experimenting. Part III of this book tries to give you much more than trial-and-error to make work more rewarding. It will discuss how you can recognize each of the intrinsic rewards so that you can gauge which intrinsic rewards need a boost. Then it will discuss the key building blocks for that intrinsic reward, so that you can identify what is missing for it. Finally, it will discuss two sets of actions you can take to enhance that building block. One set is for any leadership role you may hold—to energize people on your work team. The other set is for ways of enhancing *your own* intrinsic rewards—to make your own work more energizing and fulfilling. So there is a diagnostic framework here to help take you from any situation with low intrinsic rewards to the building blocks that are likely to be causing that situation, and then to what actions you might take—both for yourself and for team members.

My third goal has been to make this book human. I have tried to write in a fairly informal way that connects with your experience. So I'll share a few of my own experiences and ask you to think about your own, especially in the later chapters. As I wrote these sections, I have tried to imagine myself in a conversation with you where I could speak honestly about what I think you need to know and do to make work energizing and fulfilling.

One final note on the organization of the book. . . . There is a lot of drama involved in the kinds of changes this book covers—in the speed and urgency with which work has changed, in the shift from command-and-control to self-management, and in the changing motivational needs and opportunities of the new work. I have used a running "Management Tale" at the beginning of each section of the book to capture this unfolding drama.

February 2000   Kenneth W. Thomas
Monterey, California

Acknowledgments

I have had the good luck to work with people who felt passionately about intrinsic motivation. Betty Velthouse, now at the University of Michigan–Flint, first got me thinking about empowerment as a research topic when she was a Ph.D. student at the University of Pittsburgh. Walt Tymon, now at Villanova University, became a long-term research partner and lifelong friend on this adventure. Erik Jansen, my colleague at the Naval Postgraduate School, helped sort through the conceptual underbrush around this topic. It was also Erik who first suggested I write this book. I am deeply indebted to each of them for sharing ideas, enthusiasm, and support.

I am also indebted to the friends and colleagues who gave me helpful feedback on earlier drafts of this book—to Walt and Erik again, as well as Barry Leskin, Dave Jamieson, Bob Mountain, and Bev Kaye. I'd also like to thank Berrett-Koehler's reviewers for their helpful comments. I have tried to incorporate them as best I could, but remain responsible for any lapses that remain.

My wife and partner, Gail Fann Thomas, was a sounding board for many of these ideas. She also provided me with a clear model of intrinsic motivation—someone who cares passionately about doing work that makes a difference and benefits others.

I would like to thank the staff at Berrett-Koehler. Senior Editor Valerie Barth encouraged me to write about what I thought was most meaningful, and Production Director Elizabeth Swenson gave me many choices. I was fortunate to find a publishing firm that is committed to—and living—the principles I wanted to write about.

Finally, I'd like to thank the people who kept the iced tea coming at Ann Kelley's by the Lake, where I was able to reflect and write in the mornings—especially Ann, Carol, Melody, and Charlene.

PART I

The Need for New Models

A Management Tale

In earlier times, the executives turned to their most trusted advisers—the engineers and the economists—and asked how workers should be managed.

"Rationally," they replied, for such was their training. "Workers are often emotional and must be controlled. We must give them simple tasks with many rules, and watch closely to make sure they obey them."

"And will they obey?" asked the executives.

"Yes, for they are poor and we will deny them money and work if they do not."

"Very well," said the executives, and their advisers happily designed detailed Rulebooks and Compensation Systems, and built tall Hierarchies to administer them. This took time, but the world moved slowly then and there was little competition, and so their organizations prospered.

As time passed, the workers gathered into unions to protect themselves from low wages and firings. They shared in the general prosperity and became more educated. As this came to pass, they began to petition the executives that their emotional needs might better be met. This frightened the advisers, who truly believed that emotion was the doorway to Chaos. But the executives bade them modify the rules to permit modest participation and job enrichment, and their organizations prospered.

But shortly thereafter, as these things are measured, the executives beheld Great Change. The world grew small, competitors abounded in all its realms, and buyers of their wares began to demand great Speed, Quality, and Customization. As their hierarchies and rules began to fail them, the executives again turned to their advisers.

"How can we meet these demands?" they asked.

Their advisers, of course, answered, "Rationally," and fashioned the cost-cutting sword of Value Added. Wielding this sword, the executives made great slashes in their hierarchies. They also gutted the Rulebooks, that workers might better innovate and meet customer needs.

When the cutting was done, the executives found that much had changed for their workers. There were no tall hierarchies to closely monitor and direct them, nor detailed rules to comply with. *What,* the executives wondered, *will ensure that workers act responsibly now?* In answer, they heard the voices of new management gurus, who spoke of Partnership with workers, and the need for workers to feel Passion for the work and to derive Fulfillment from it. And the executives heard in this message the truth of their own energy for work.

The executives then turned to their trusted advisers. "How can we manage for Passion and Fulfillment?" they asked.

"We cannot answer that question," replied the advisers, "for it is not rational."

1

The Shift from Compliance to Partnership

It is hard to grasp how quickly and dramatically the worker's role has changed. It was only in 1991 that the word *empowerment* began appearing in the *Business Periodicals Index,* and some writers have already discarded it.[1] Few organizations still use *subordinate* to describe workers. Even the word *employee* has given way to *associate* in several Fortune 100 organizations. These word changes signal a profound shift that contemporary managers and workers are trying to come to terms with.

From the beginning of the twentieth century until quite recently, it was reasonably accurate to think of workers' roles in terms of compliance.[2] *Sound management* meant simplifying work tasks, producing thick rulebooks, and building tall hierarchies to make sure that workers complied with the rules. This was command-and-control management in bureaucratic organizations. It was supported by the economics of the times: in a stable environment with heavy demand, the rules produced standardized products and services that met customer needs, and the simplified work meant lower pay and training costs for workers. And generations of managers, workers, and academics had time to get used to this reality.

There were some challenges to this mind-set in the 1970s, when participative management and job enrichment began making inroads. Demonstration projects showed that managers could sometimes relax constraints to allow workers more "choice and voice," and that gains in motivation and work quality would offset higher wages. But the economic advantages were controversial, and the dramatic experiments were done mostly in Europe under government-sponsored programs to enhance the quality of work life. So there was limited enthusiasm in U.S. boardrooms. Participative management and job enrichment, in Richard Walton's phrase, stayed a "local option" for managers with certain leadership styles.[3]

By the 1990s, however, technology had changed the economic equation. Telecommunications created a truly global marketplace, with intense competition and the need for quicker responses. Customers demanded greater reliability and customized products and services. Inside the organization, computers and automation changed the nature of the work, reducing the number of low-skilled jobs and increasing the need for worker judgment. Computers gave workers access to the information that enabled decentralized decisions. These conditions, as Warren Bennis had predicted years before, are bringing about "the death of bureaucracy."[4] The tall hierarchies are becoming not only unnecessary but an actual interference with workers' ability to respond quickly to customer needs. The same is true of the detailed rules. One by one, Fortune 500 organizations have announced large layoffs of middle managers, and CEOs have condensed rulebooks down to a few guiding principles.

In this new environment, it is no longer a question of middle managers' *allowing* workers more choice and participation. Many of the middle management positions have been eliminated, and the organization needs its workers to take on much of the supervisory and managerial roles. Instead of complying with detailed rules, workers are now asked to be proactive problem solvers. They must make adjustments, coordinate with other organizational players, innovate, and initiate changes. Workers are becoming strategic partners of top management, deciding the actions needed at the grassroots level to meet the organization's goals.

It is hard to draw precise boundaries around these changes. Some industries and job types come immediately to mind—"high tech" and "knowledge workers." But the new work is not confined to particular industries and job classifications. Because of global competition and technological change, virtually all organizations are under pressure to better harness the intelligence and commitment of their work forces. It seems that no segment is exempt—including manufacturing and the military. Fewer and fewer organizations can afford to use people only for compliance. Stanford professor Jeffrey Pfeffer has argued that using human resources well has become an important source of competitive advantage.[5] As competition and technological change continue to accelerate, it is likely to become a requirement for survival. Jack Welch, CEO of General Electric, put it this way: "I think any company . . . has got to find a way to engage the mind of every single employee. . . . If you're not thinking all the time about making every person more valuable, you don't have a chance. What's the alternative? Wasted minds? Uninvolved people? A labor force that's angry or bored? That doesn't make sense."[6]

With all these changes, then, it is clear that today's workers need to be treated differently than in past decades. They have earned somewhat higher wages. However, the most significant differences go beyond economics. The new work role is more psychologically demanding in terms of its complexity and judgment, and requires a much deeper level of commitment. While economic rewards were pretty good for buying compliance, gaining commitment is a far different matter. Many recent books have addressed the new leadership and the new management. These books provide useful clues on the motivational needs and opportunities of the new work. However, they have not tackled those issues head on. This book focuses squarely on that important topic.

Let's begin by looking at the mainstays of the traditional approach to motivation—extrinsic rewards and rational-economic assumptions. After all, the first step in a new understanding of motivation is to understand the limitations and baggage that came with the traditional approach, and why it is no longer enough.

2

Extrinsic Rewards
Are No Longer Enough

When organizations wanted only compliance from workers, they bought it with money and other tangible benefits. In the language of motivation theory, these are *extrinsic* rewards. Extrinsic rewards don't come from the work itself, they are doled out by supervisors to ensure that work is done properly and that the rules are followed. They include things like salaries, bonuses, commissions, perks, benefits, and cash awards.

Extrinsic rewards were an easy solution to motivation in the compliance era. They were *possible*. The tall hierarchies allowed managers to supervise workers closely, so that they knew when rules were being followed and could give or withhold rewards accordingly. And they were enough. Organizations only needed to buy rote behavior, not commitment and initiative. They didn't need to appeal to workers' passions, or even enlist much of their intelligence. Finally, they were all management had to offer. With the simplified work and the constraining rules and procedures, few intrinsic rewards were possible.

Consider the daily experience of a compliance-era job with its extrinsic rewards and few intrinsic rewards. Nearly everyone has had one—hopefully only for summer jobs or early in your career. Mine involved a white-collar laboratory job. There was some challenge in learning the detailed job rules at first, but that didn't take long. Then I settled into a boring routine, and much of my work behavior went on automatic pilot. If I had a question, I had to ask the supervisor. My mind wandered. I found myself watching the clock before breaks and toward the end of the day. I looked forward to anything that broke the monotony, and started to invent mental games. I put unnecessary creativity into things that might give me satisfaction, like the quality of my printing. The only excitement involved a standing card game during the lunch break. I had to drag myself to work each morning, but went because I needed the money.

Intrinsic Rewards

With today's work, on the other hand, motivational issues are more complex and demanding. Close supervision and detailed rules are no longer as possible. Workers now need to be more self-managing. Self-management, in turn, requires more initiative and commitment, which depend on deeper passions and satisfactions than extrinsic rewards can offer. Finally (and fortunately), the new work has the potential for much richer, *intrinsic* rewards. Intrinsic rewards come to workers directly from the work they do—satisfactions like pride of workmanship or the sense that they are helping a customer.

Since the new work is more like managerial work, I'll try to evoke the feel of that sort of work by capturing the experience of effective managers I know. Above all, they are energized by the work itself and feel passionate about it. They see their work as making a significant difference and believe in what they are trying to accomplish. Usually, they see themselves helping people in some way. They get satisfaction from situations they have handled well and are proud of creative innovations and ideas they have come up with. Of course there are challenges and some setbacks, but overall, they are fulfilled and rewarded by the work. Far from having to drag themselves to work, they take the work home—physically, or by thinking about it. In fact, they often find it necessary to ration the time they allow themselves to work, so as not to sacrifice other areas of their life.

In the new work, then, intrinsic motivation is crucial. Does this mean that extrinsic rewards have become unimportant? Of course not. Some early research on intrinsic motivation had an either-or flavor, believing that extrinsic rewards would drive out intrinsic motivation. But later research shows that the two kinds of rewards often support each other.[1] It is helpful to think of the relationship in terms of foreground and background. Extrinsic rewards come into the foreground when workers are short on funds or benefits, when issues of unfairness arise, and when workers face major choices. They fade into the background the rest of the time, and intrinsic rewards take the foreground in day-to-day work.

For example, I recently interviewed many army reserve soldiers.[2] It was clear that salary and benefits were important for many reservists when they decided to join, or to "re-up" when their contract expired (along with patriotism and other factors). After they made the decision to join, however, they were faced each day with the reality of the work they had taken on, and their energy for that work depended on the intrinsic rewards they got from it. The same is true in any job. Work is seldom a short sprint for a reward. Over the long haul, people need intrinsic rewards to keep going and to perform at their peak. Despite your best intentions, you can only gut it out so long if you don't enjoy the journey itself!

Intrinsic Rewards and Retention

This gets us to the crucial role of intrinsic rewards in keeping good workers. A number of theorists have noted that the informal "psychological contract" between organizations and workers has shifted.[3] Today's organizations can no longer offer guaranteed employment and a pension in return for worker loyalty and obedience. And workers with dull jobs are less willing to grit their teeth and hang on for the mere possibility of an eventual pension. Workers have been forced to take more responsibility for their own careers, going where the work is rewarding and where they can develop skills that will guarantee their employability—in whatever organization. This mobility and "free agency" has created greater competition for skilled workers between organizations. Good workers have more choices than before, and are more likely to use them.

As workers have become more likely to leave unrewarding jobs, the loss of good workers has become less tolerable. With global competition, few organizations can afford the cost of recruiting and training replacements for many of their workers. The major accounting firms, for example, can no longer afford to replace the many workers who join them to learn the business and get professionally certified, only to leave for more interesting jobs with other firms. Even the military, which traditionally fills a job-training role for society, is struggling to reduce turnover in an era of tighter money. The army, for example, can buy a large truck for the cost of replacing each trained reservist who quits! And the obvious economic costs do not include the setbacks to projects, the lost corporate knowledge, and the general disruption to working relationships.

Managing for intrinsic rewards, then, has become the crucial next step in keeping good workers. Organizations have had generations to develop their extrinsic reward systems. To be sure, some refinements can still be made. For example, it will be important to keep adjusting benefits to the needs of new workers—providing things like flextime, flexplace, childcare, and eldercare. However, most of the high-grade ore in extrinsic reward systems has already been mined, and fine-tuning will lead to smaller improvements in retention. We are now at the point where the biggest gains will come from systematically improving intrinsic rewards—making the work itself more fulfilling and energizing so that workers don't want to leave it.

3

Getting Beyond
Rational–Economic
Assumptions

If you are like me, the notion that you are energized or deenergized by your work fits your experience—it rings true at a gut level. When I first heard this idea, however, I remember that it had a flavor of New Age mysticism: psychic energy? I now realize that the idea seemed strange to me because it did not fit the rational-economic model that has long dominated thinking about work motivation. Management had several generations to perfect the motivation of compliance. Over this time, the rational-economic thinking that underlies compliance motivation became so ingrained that it seemed self-evident.

Herb Simon, the Nobel prize–winning economist, described the rational model of decision making as follows.[1] When people make choices, they first identify their alternatives. They then consider the likely outcomes of each alternative and the desirability ("utility") of those outcomes. Finally, they choose the alternative that would lead to the most desirable outcome. In simpler terms, *the assumption is that people choose behaviors based on their anticipated consequences.* This is pretty familiar stuff: it is the foundation of cost/benefit analysis and pervades management education. Even in the most psychological of management courses, the dominant motivational model has been "expectancy theory," which explains worker motivation in this way.[2]

For most of us who received this sort of training, the rational model became an automatic way of understanding behavior. And for a long time, it

10

worked: the rational model fit the needs of compliance-era management very well. With workers choosing to attend work, to produce, and to follow the rules largely because of extrinsic outcomes, managers could use the rational model to design reward systems to "incentivize" those behaviors—trying to make sure that desired behaviors would result in economic rewards.

Now, with intrinsic rewards more important, we need to loosen the grip of the rational-economic model on our thinking by recognizing its limitations. Economics is powerful in the consistency of its rational model and in its mathematical tools. However, it is more vulnerable in the fit between its assumptions and actual human behavior. Here, it screens out some motivational realities that are vital to intrinsic motivation.

Consider the following points about intrinsic motivation that go beyond rational-economic thinking.

Point 1. People care about more than money and self-interest at work.

One familiar complaint about economic thinking, of course, is that it focuses on personal economic gain. Theorists like Ed Schein at MIT and the late Abe Maslow pointed out that workers have "higher-order" personal needs that also shape behavior.[3] Even Maslow's familiar needs hierarchy (from physiological needs to self-actualization), it was pointed out later, is phrased in terms of personal needs. Some of the most significant work rewards come from transpersonal motives, such as helping others. For example, I often do an exercise in which I ask people to recall when they were feeling particularly great about their work. They often pick times when people depended upon them and they were able to come through. Try this exercise yourself; it's an eye opener.

If you stick with traditional economic assumptions about work, you're also likely to assume that working is a *cost* for workers. If you buy into that assumption, it leads to a number of other conclusions that make it hard to think intelligently about intrinsic rewards. It suggests, for example, that workers don't want to work, want leisure instead, and will retire as soon as they can afford it. All these conclusions appear to be extremely questionable for the new work, and can be dangerously self-fulfilling. It isn't true that work is a cost. *Unrewarding* work is a cost. Rewarding work, on the other hand, is also a good—something one seeks and "consumes." People have a desire to be engaged in meaningful work—to be doing something they experience as worthwhile and fulfilling. While leisure is welcome in moderate doses—especially after long periods of work—it gets old by itself. People need tasks to structure their days and to provide purpose—something of significance to engage them.

As I was writing this book, the AARP released a study showing that a large portion of older workers plan to keep working even though they have enough money to retire. In the same week, another news item involved thirteen machinists who won a huge Powerball lottery and announced that they would remain on their jobs because they "enjoy working there." Clearly, there are important rewards other than money that people get from work.

Point 2. Intrinsic motivation involves rewards you are getting right now.

Another limitation of the rational-economic model comes from the idea of rationality itself. The rational model does not include the experience of getting or enjoying rewards! It's basically a decision-making model. It involves desiring rewarding outcomes in the future, figuring out how to maximize them, and deciding to strive to get them. But it is not about whether or not you are getting rewarded now—whether you are enjoying your work. In the rational model, the present moment is a time to calculate and make decisions so that the future can be desirable, and to strive to attain that desirable future. Rationality is based on a logic of delayed gratification, which feeds all too well into our culture's puritanism and Protestant work ethic: "This is serious stuff we're doing here; the future is at stake." This is a pretty barren theoretical landscape for spotting intrinsic rewards!

In technical terms, economics is driven by *prospective rationality*. To understand how the work experience can be energizing, it is more useful to use models driven by *reinforcement*. Reinforcement models focus on the rewards (reinforcements) that one is getting from one's work, and how these rewards energize (reinforce) continued work behavior. In a reinforcement model, then, *feeling energized by one's work is simply the experience of getting rewards directly from the work*. There is nothing mystical about it. The basic question I will address in this book, then, is whether or not people are getting rewards from their work now.

Point 3. Intrinsic rewards are about emotions.

Consider how emotions are treated in the rational model. Emotions are sanitized into your "utilities" for future events. In the present moment, emotions are seen as a threat to the rationality of decision making, and are therefore to be controlled. Emotions, by definition, are nonrational, and the fear is that they will lead to irrational behavior—that is, to choices that reduce future outcomes. In reinforcement models, on the other hand, emotions are at the core of motivation. Basically, *intrinsic rewards are those things about the work that feel good*—that generate positive emotions. To harness intrinsic motivation is to understand these emotions and to amplify them.

Point 4. Doing "the right thing" makes people feel good.

Finally, consider how the rational model treats moral standards of behavior—standards like "tell the truth." In the rational model, behaviors are considered means to an end, and are chosen solely in terms of their expected consequences. In that model, quite literally, the ends justify the means, and moral issues such as "should I cheat on my taxes?" are settled on the basis of "what will happen if I do?" For example, I recall a classroom example from the distant past on corporate bribery. The economics professor led us through the intricacies of this decision. Students' reactions of "that would be wrong!" got translated into "how bad would you feel?" and then into "how much profit would be necessary to make up for your guilt?" I remember thinking that this line of reasoning might mean that we had already abandoned the high moral ground and, as in the old joke, were now simply haggling about the price of our virtue. Business schools work harder now to stress ethics in their curricula, but I have the nagging suspicion that it is the rational model itself that contributes to much of the difficulty. As sociologists like Amatai Etzioni have pointed out, people not only strive for desirable outcomes, they also try to *do the right thing,* even though it occasionally costs them to do so.[4] Some intrinsic rewards involve a sense of honor from doing the right thing morally or ethically, independent of the personal consequences.

To sum up, getting beyond the limitations of the rational-economic model makes it possible to understand how intrinsic rewards can energize work. To understand what those rewards are, it is necessary to look at the nature of the new work.

PART II

The Nature of the New Work

A Management Tale, continued ...

So the executives took their question to the new management gurus and consultants: "How can we manage for Passion and Fulfillment?"

Some of the executives were skeptical that this could be done. "We have our doubts in this matter, for, if truth be spoken, it looks to us that workers must simply do More. For they must not only perform their labors; now they must also decide the course of their labors."

"How will they make such decisions?" asked the consultants.

"They must be guided by Purposes, of course," replied the executives.

"Ah!" said the consultants. "Purpose is the key, for their work has been without it. People are purposeful creatures," they continued, "and need to know that their lives contain adventures toward worthy Purposes. But their work has been empty of this. *You* have been the Keepers of the Purpose. For you, there have always been challenges as you strived toward a Purpose. For the workers, there was only the doing of small things. Yes, you must share the Purpose with the workers, that they might better share in these adventures."

"Very well," said the executives, and they began by speaking to the workers of Profit and Market Share. But they found that these goals did not inspire passion in the workers. The workers, they learned, needed purposes that rang of nobler aims—of Contribution and of Betterment.

So the executives reached deeper into their own purposes. They had learned that their successes came from bettering the conditions of their Customers, and from the Quality of their goods and services. These purposes gave them pride, and they offered them to the workers as nobler things for which to strive.

The workers responded to these purposes. "Ah, yes," they thought, "helping Customers and working with Quality. This is a more worthy endeavor. There is opportunity for fulfillment and honor in such work."

So the executives crafted Vision Statements that emphasized Contribution to Customers and Quality, and they hoped that all would be well. But they found that managing for Passion and Fulfillment was not so simple a thing as they had wished. Their Vision Statements inspired hope and meaning at first, but often rang hollow in time—like unkept promises.

4

Purposeful Work

To understand intrinsic motivation and the new work, it is necessary to reexamine the nature of work itself.

What Is Work, Anyway?

I invite you to take a moment to examine your own assumptions about work. Work is made up of *tasks*. What words or phrases come to mind when you try to define what a task is? If that is too general a question, then pick a specific task in your work team and think how you would describe it to a new team member.

I've learned that there are two very different ways of answering that question. The first way reflects the traditional, activity-centered notion of work. It says that tasks are made up of *activities* (behaviors) that a worker needs to perform. So if you were explaining flight attendants' jobs, for example, you would mention things like giving safety instructions, serving meals and beverages, and distributing pillows. This is the way most of us were trained to think about workers' jobs. It is a notion of work that fit the compliance era very well, since compliance is about following behavioral directions.

The other way of answering the question involves a more purpose-centered view of work. It says that tasks are most fundamentally defined by the purposes they serve. If you were explaining flight attendants' jobs in a purpose-centered way, for example, you might say they are there to keep passengers safe, comfortable, and satisfied. Or you might mention the purposes as a way of explaining the task activities: giving safety demonstrations and enforcing FAA rules to promote safety, providing food and bedding for passenger comfort, and generally trying to keep passengers satisfied.

These purpose-centered answers reflect a fundamental insight about work tasks. Tasks are made up of more than the activities people perform. After all, those task activities only exist because someone chose them as a way of accomplishing a purpose. *Tasks, then, are sets of activities directed toward a purpose.* Betty Velthouse and I offered that insight in an article ten years ago, and I am still amazed at its importance.[1]

Rediscovering the role of purpose in work is key to understanding the new work and the motivation of today's workers. Without a clear notion of purpose, workers cannot make intelligent choices about work activities, and they are also deprived of a sense of the meaningfulness of their work. So, if you and others in your organization are still thinking about work in an activity-centered way, you'll have some rethinking to do.

Two Important Facts about Purposes

Before I can talk about the reemergence of task purposes in work, it is necessary to explain two things about them. First, task purposes generally involve events that are external to workers' jobs. That is, most task purposes involve outcomes that occur not to the worker, but to some customers (internal or external) in the worker's environment. There are some exceptions involving secondary tasks. For example, my task of cleaning off my desk is aimed at allowing me to better accomplish my main task purposes. But those main purposes involve meeting the needs of book publishers, readers, students, and research sponsors. It is environmental needs like this that create jobs in the first place. Meeting those needs, and having a positive impact on one's environment, is also what gives tasks their significance or meaningfulness.

The second point is that achieving task purposes is not totally under a worker's control and involves inevitable uncertainties. Since they are external to workers' jobs, task purposes depend not only upon workers' activities, but on outside events as well. For example, flight attendants' purpose of keeping passengers satisfied depends on passengers' moods, flight delays, turbulence, and the behavior of other passengers. Likewise, a forest ranger's success in keeping wildlife healthy depends on factors like naturally occurring diseases, lightning-started forest fires, and the behavior of campers and hunters. It is the fact of these uncertainties that provides much of the challenge and suspense involved in accomplishing task purposes, and that produces much of the satisfaction in their accomplishment.

How Purpose Got Removed from Work

If purposes are fundamental parts of tasks, how did they get separated from traditional notions of work? The answer goes back to the early twentieth century, when the industrial era was blooming. It was then that so-called *scientific* approaches to management began to develop, largely to meet the demands of the new phenomenon of mass production—as epitomized by auto assembly lines. The environment of the early twentieth century was considerably more stable and predictable than today's. That is, its uncertainties were more manageable for the organization. This meant that organizations could largely coordinate their tasks using two simple devices: centralized, hierarchical control and detailed rules and procedures.[2]

Let's start with centralized, hierarchical control. Because uncertainties were relatively manageable, managers could take on the responsibility for handling them. In effect, they walled workers off from the environment and its uncertainties. For decades, it was considered sound management practice to "buffer" workers from potentially disruptive environmental events and to "absorb" uncertainty on their behalf, and this language was reflected in the classic works on management.[3] (Note how paternalistic this language sounds today, as management consultants like Peter Block have pointed out.[4]) Managers essentially took over the decision making involved in handling uncertainties in order to achieve the task purpose. They became the "keepers of the purpose." Knowing about task purposes and their accomplishment became unnecessary for workers.

Without a knowledge of purpose, of course, workers could not make intelligent decisions about which task activities to perform, or how. So management had to provide directions on what activities to perform and how to perform them—in the form of detailed rules and procedures. Worker judgment itself was seen as a source of uncertainty that needed to be controlled, so these rules and procedures were also used to systematically eliminate choice from jobs. Industrial engineers determined the optimal sequence of activities needed in a worker's job, and the optimal way of performing those activities—often down to individual arm movements. Frederick Winslow Taylor championed this "Scientific Management" approach to job design, also referred to as "time and motion" or "efficiency" work.[5] In short, work tasks came to be defined solely in terms of behavioral activities, and those activities were prescribed through detailed rules and procedures. Managers enforced compliance with those rules and procedures through close supervision and extrinsic rewards and punishments.

This treatment of workers seemed like the natural order of things during the industrial era. Machinery was celebrated as the great enabler of efficiency and productivity. Engineers became influential voices in organizations, and organizations themselves came to be viewed as machines. Managers tried to run their organizations like machines—rationally, predictably, impersonally, and efficiently. Their emphasis on centralized control and elaborate rules came to be called "machine bureaucracy." It was easy, by extension, to think of workers as imperfect pieces, or cogs, within the organizational machinery. The classic Charlie Chaplin film *Modern Times* provided a memorable portrayal of this assumption. Economists, with their emphasis on rationality and extrinsic rewards, provided further support for the engineers' views.

Why Purpose Is Back at Work

Bureaucratic principles about management were so ingrained that it took a great deal of research in the second half of the twentieth century to show that there were significant exceptions. Less bureaucratic forms of organization, it developed, were better for some kinds of technologies and environments where there were greater uncertainties.[6] But now, at the beginning of the twenty-first century, these "exceptions" have become the rule. The environment that was so stable a hundred years ago is now fast-paced and unpredictable—what Peter Vaill at George Washington University aptly calls "permanent whitewater."[7] The world is smaller and organizations must respond on-line to developments in a truly global economy. Technological innovation continues to accelerate, as does the rate of development of new products. Customers demand greater customization of products and services, along with faster deliveries. Even mass-production organizations are scrambling to redesign their processes and to continually improve their quality.

The upshot is that the number and complexity of the uncertainties facing organizations have overwhelmed the capacity of bureaucratic management. The hierarchy can no longer absorb most of these uncertainties or buffer workers from them, so that the wall between workers and the organization's environment has come crashing down. Organizations need workers to take active responsibility for handling more and more of the uncertainties involved in the accomplishment of their purposes. So organizations have been forced to flatten their hierarchies and push decision making down to workers. Workers are called on to adapt to customers' needs, simplify and improve organizational processes, coordinate with other workers and teams, and initiate ideas for new products and services. In short, organizations now depend on workers to use their own judgment and to make many of the decisions formerly made by managers alone.

As decision making has become less centralized, rules and procedures are being dramatically reduced. After all, much of their rationale was to reduce and control worker choice, and organizations now need to give workers the space to make intelligent choices. Consider the old refrain that countless customers heard when encountering bureaucratic requirements that made no sense in their case: "Sorry, I'm just following the rules." That line is no longer acceptable in today's business climate, and is being replaced by "Let's see what I can do to help." Flight attendants are generally free now to hand out drinks or snacks during long on-ground delays, for example, instead of sticking to a strict schedule. Likewise, hotel receptionists are increasingly given the leeway to reduce charges to make up for service deficiencies reported by customers. In this new environment, then, it is widely recognized that employee empowerment requires a pushing down of choice and authority to workers to allow intelligent decisions.

The point that I want to emphasize here is that all these changes also require that a strong sense of purpose gets put back into workers' jobs.

Workers simply cannot make intelligent choices without having clear task purposes. Workers must also be committed to those purposes. For, as mentioned earlier, the greater judgment of the new work requires a deeper personal commitment than did the old compliance work. For these and other reasons, career counselor Richard Leider has suggested calling the new era the "Age of Purpose."[8]

The Human Need for Purpose

Fortunately, organizations' needs for committed, purposeful work fit an intense human need for purpose. It is the purpose aspect of the new work that most enlists our commitment and stirs our passions. Our workdays may be structured by our work activities, but those activities are given meaning and significance by the purposes they serve. Much of the color in our lives comes from the drama, challenge, struggle—and hopefully the triumph—of handling the uncertainties involved in accomplishing those purposes.

There is a great deal of evidence that people are hardwired to care about purposes. We seem to need to see ourselves as going somewhere—as being on a journey in pursuit of a significant purpose. In *The Hero with a Thousand Faces,* the late Joseph Campbell reported that virtually all cultures have parallel myths about heroic journeys.[9] These journeys involve dramatic difficulties, dangers, periods of despair, and eventual success—always in the service of a worthy purpose. These myths, then, seem to capture an essential part of the human experience.

There is also much evidence that people suffer when they lack purpose. Clinical studies show that people deteriorate in various ways without purpose. This insight first showed up in the survival of concentration camp internees,[10] but also seems to be a factor in the survival and well-being of military prisoners of war, people in nursing homes, and even retirees. In the 1960s, the French Existentialist movement also drew attention to the psychological emptiness that comes from a lack of purpose. Philosophers like Sartre and Camus pointed out that, without purpose, life becomes meaningless and people experience a sense of alienation and "angst." Camus captured this sense of meaninglessness vividly in *The Myth of Sisyphus.*[11] Sisyphus was a king in Greek mythology who had so offended the gods that he was condemned to roll a large stone up a steep hill in Hades, only to watch it roll down and endlessly repeat this cycle. This Greek version of hell, then, was essentially a demanding but meaningless activity with no purpose.

The lack of purpose in the compliance era, then, had significant psychological costs for workers. But generations of workers came to accept this as the nature of work. In his book *Working,* Studs Terkel used the memorable phrase "a Monday through Friday sort of dying" to refer to these costs at their worst.[12] Compliance-era work was a bit like Sisyphus's toil, except that you could go home in the evening and take the weekend off. Workers came to think of this sort of work as a kind of necessary evil (or devil's bargain)—forty to sixty hours a week of meaningless labor in exchange for economic survival. Work was considered an economic cost that left you depleted. It was something to survive rather than enjoy—something to withdraw from emotionally, to numb out from and get through.

In contrast, today's workers—and especially knowledge workers—tend to expect their work to be at least somewhat meaningful and rewarding. They are more educated than workers of the preceding era, have a higher standard of living, and see more opportunities for meaning in the new work.[13] So today's work force and the new work combine to produce a growing demand for meaningful work. This demand is becoming a powerful force in the new job market. There have been a number of recent books aimed at workers who want to change jobs to find work that better serves the purposes they care about. Organizations now find themselves competing to attract and retain workers on the basis of the meaningfulness of their work. I live close enough to Silicon Valley to hear the radio ads stressing the opportunity to move to an organization that offers "exciting projects" that "make a difference."

Discovering Purpose-Centered Leadership

As the work environment and worker expectations have changed, our understanding of leadership has gone through a dramatic paradigm shift. Virtually all the compliance-era models of leadership talked about the twin concerns of *task* and *people.* Which should you emphasize and when? Looking back, however, it seems that most of that research was done on first-line supervisors at a time when managers buffered workers from environmental uncertainties. So the emphasis on tasks was really a concern with how to perform task activities properly—the old compliance-era focus. Likewise, the motivational assumptions behind the research were about exchanges or transactions of extrinsic rewards for performing those activities. These models are now called "transactional" leadership.[14]

By the late 1970s and early 1980s, however, it was clear that these models were no longer adequate. They didn't work for higher-level leadership, and they didn't work when workers had to adapt and change in response to environmental uncertainties. What was missing, of course, was any mention of an overriding and meaningful task purpose.

In the late 1970s, the political scientist James McGregor Burns published an influential study of U.S. presidents who had inspired effective national change.[15] What he found, essentially, was that these presidents had held out a worthy purpose around which the nation could rally. These presidents were also able to articulate a compelling vision of what the future would be like if that purpose were met. The purpose and vision, then, provided a target that could align the efforts of different people to solve problems and cooperate. At the same time, the compelling vision was a strong motivational force that inspired people. Burns emphasized that these meaningful purposes appealed to people's higher nature, rather than to their "lower" needs for self-interest and extrinsic rewards. He called this form of leadership "transformational."

Burns's purpose-centered approach to leadership was soon adapted by management researchers and practitioners. Since the 1980s, there have been a wealth of books on transformational, inspirational, or visionary leadership.[16] The new purpose-centered models of leadership now apply not only to top managers, but to team leaders at all organizational levels. Purpose-centered leadership gives workers the information they need to make intelligent decisions and also provides an intrinsically rewarding sense of meaningfulness for their work. Even the rather hierarchical U.S. military has shifted leadership practices to emphasize purpose-centered leadership. Written orders now begin with a "Commander's Intent" that spells out the purpose behind an order. Knowing that purpose makes the activities more meaningful, but also allows individuals to improvise to better accomplish the purpose when they encounter unexpected circumstances. (I will be discussing purpose-centered leadership in more detail in Part III of this book.)

Organizational Vision Statements

Organizational statements of vision followed from purpose-centered leadership, and are now very common. Again, their purpose is both to guide decision making and to gain commitment to a common purpose. Because they are aimed at gaining commitment rather than compliance, these vision statements can't be enacted by fiat and simply pushed down through the organization. You can't delegate commitment, after all—you have to find a purpose that inspires it. So vision statements have pulled organizational planning in new directions where values and emotion play a stronger role.

As Burns had learned with U.S. presidents, corporate CEOs found that not all purposes are equal. Some evoke deeper passions than others. In particular, workers are seldom inspired by economic purposes involving profit—unless the company's welfare is threatened. Rather, inspiration generally comes from deeper values and higher purposes. A good vision statement forces management to dig into the fundamental values that underlie the organization's culture—to understand what the organization stands for.[17] Common themes here are service to customers, quality, and innovation—things that people in the organization take pride in. The organization's vision, then, is a statement of an exciting future that would be meaningful and worthy as judged by those values.

In this way, purpose-centered leadership and workers' needs for meaning have become a force for redefining organizational goals. Although profits and market share remain important, the trend is no longer to see them as paramount. Two recent studies of organizations that had been highly successful over a long period found that such organizations had core ideologies emphasizing "more than profits."[18] One of those researchers used the following analogy to describe the status of economic goals: "They need profits in the same way as any living being needs oxygen. It is a necessity to stay alive, but it is not the purpose of life."[19] Peter Block has argued that purposes such as customer service and quality are not only more meaningful for workers but are also what put organizations closer to the marketplace to begin with, and are therefore what take care of financial issues.[20]

In summary, then, it's clear that the new work is more purposeful than compliance-era work. To more fully describe the new work, the next chapter looks at the steps today's workers must go through to achieve those purposes—the process of self-management.

5

Self-Management in the Pursuit of Purpose

So what is the nature of this purposeful new work? You'll probably miss it if you only look at the visible activities or behaviors of this work. You will see only tremendous variety—bookkeeping, carpentry, counseling, telephone sales, and so on. The common core requirements of the new work aren't behavioral at all—at least in the traditional way we think of overt, behavioral actions. They involve the mental events that direct those actions toward a purpose.

Consider the way managers talk about the new work. It involves "working smart," "using judgment," "taking responsibility," and "applying your intelligence" toward the organization's purposes. Again, these are mental events. Academics use fancier words to describe this purposive mental activity: *self-regulating, self-controlling,* and *self-managing.* I prefer the term *self-managing* because it conveys the idea that workers now do much of what managers used to do for them.

Worker Self-Management?

The idea that industrial workers were capable of mentally managing their own tasks would probably have provoked laughter or bewilderment early in the twentieth century. Even the psychology of that era seemed to exclude it.

For much of the twentieth century, psychology was dominated by *behaviorism,* as epitomized by the work of B. F. Skinner.[1] Behaviorists maintained that only visible behavior was a proper subject of scientific study. Human purposes, decision making, and thoughts were regarded as elusive "black box" events that were not "real" in a scientific sense and had no value in explaining behavior. Skinner and his associates believed that behavior was determined entirely by external events—specifically by external reinforcements. Their psychology, then, was largely a science of behavioral control via extrinsic rewards and punishments. In that way, the psychology of the early twentieth century provided scientific support for the compliance-era treatment of workers, and was helpful for fine-tuning the use of extrinsic rewards and punishments. When should you use punishments, and when rewards? Should you reward a desired behavior each time it occurred, or more infrequently?

Looking back, Skinner's science was not a human psychology at all. It looked for basic causal laws that fit all animals—even those with primitive nervous systems. Skinner experimented with rats and generalized to people and other organisms. Even flatworms, it turned out, could be trained to turn left if you shocked them for turning right! This was hardly a science to appreciate workers' capacity for decision making. It wasn't that Skinner was factually wrong about the effects of rewards and punishments on behavior, but rather that his science screened out much of the product of human evolution! The psychology of the compliance era, then, contributed to the gulf between managers and workers. Managers experienced themselves as thinking human beings but were advised to think of workers as unthinking creatures whose behavior needed to be controlled with rewards and punishments. In Herzberg's words, managers were encouraged to act as though they were "animal trainers."[2]

Fortunately, behaviorism went into steep decline in the last half of the twentieth century. In its place, *cognitive psychology* developed to study the effects of thoughts, assumptions, and intentions in shaping human behavior. Especially in the last twenty years, this work has demonstrated that people are inherently self-regulating—that they commit to goals or purposes, monitor their attainment, make adjustments, and learn.[3] So contemporary psychology has now developed a more solid foundation for understanding the self-management involved in the new work. In doing so, it has also helped bridge the gulf between managers and workers.

What's Involved in Self-Management?

Figure 5.1 shows a flow chart that Erik Jansen and I developed to show the essential events in self-management.[4] The oval represents visible *task activities*—overt task behaviors like planting flowers, grinding lenses, or taking orders over the telephone. The four rectangles are the *self-management events* that direct that behavior toward a purpose. Like most flow charts, the diagram oversimplifies what is often an intuitive and messy process. However, it is useful in fleshing out the key parts of self-management.

The solid arrows in the figure show the main sequence of events, from left to right. Self-management begins when you commit to a meaningful purpose. You then choose activities to accomplish the purpose. As you perform those activities, you monitor the competence of that performance to

FIGURE 5.1 The Self-Management Process

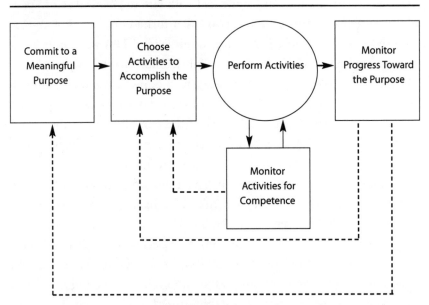

Note: Oval represents overt task behavior. Boxes represent internal (cognitive) self-management events that direct overt behavior. Dotted lines represent feedback effects.

Source: Adapted from Kenneth W. Thomas, Erik Jansen, and Walter G. Tymon Jr., "Navigating in the Realm of Theory: An Empowering View of Construct Development," *Research in Organizational Change and Development,* 10 (1997): 1–30. Reprinted by permission of the publisher.

make sure that it is adequate. Finally, you monitor progress toward accomplishing the task purpose to make sure that the activities are having the intended effect and actually moving the purpose forward.

For example, consider a self-managing gardener who works for a landscaping firm. The gardener commits to planting a flower garden that will delight a customer. She chooses which flowers to plant and where to plant them. As she plants them, she monitors her behavior to make sure the plants have proper soil, that their root balls are properly covered, and that they receive enough water. Periodically, she checks with the customer to make sure that the customer is actually delighted with how the garden is taking shape.

The dotted lines in the figure are feedback effects. They represent adjustments and learnings during the course of a task. For example, if activities aren't being performed well enough, you can adjust your performance or, if that doesn't work, you can choose other activities. Likewise, if the purpose isn't being accomplished, you can look for new activities that will move the task forward.

The next sections go into more detail about each of the events in self-management, to build a better understanding of what today's work requires.

Committing to a Meaningful Purpose

Without commitment to a purpose, there would be no point in the remaining events. There would be no reason to make choices, care about the competence of one's work behavior, or keep track of progress. In many ways, then, this commitment drives the entire self-management process.

So what is commitment? Commitment to a purpose is inspired by the pull of a worthy, desirable purpose. But commitment is clearly more than desiring or hoping that the purpose will be achieved. It is a decision to take personal responsibility for making it happen. Let me spell out this distinction, because it is important. Much decision making is activity-centered rather than purpose-centered. In activity-centered decision making, we decide to perform behaviors with the hope that they will accomplish a purpose. The purpose is in the background as a desire, intention, or aim. We perform the activities and see what happens. If those activities don't achieve the purpose, we are disappointed, but that is sometimes the nature of life, and we move on to another task.

In purpose-centered decision making, in contrast, we commit to a purpose, and the activities are in the background. That is, we're not entirely sure how we will accomplish the purpose. The decision is basically to find the activities needed to deal with the uncertainties involved. Subject to our moral code and our other commitments, we are deciding to do whatever is needed to accomplish the purpose.

The nature of commitment became clearest to me when I approached marriage, so I'll use that as an analogy. I could have made a "reasonable effort" to make the relationship succeed and then waited to see how well that worked. But I realized that this wait-and-see approach would have real consequences: it would make it less likely that the relationship would succeed, and would also make it less likely that my wife-to-be would commit to making it work. I realized that I already knew enough about my future wife to make a commitment, and that I needed to do so. So I made the commitment—to myself and to her. And we both began to use the language of commitment: "We will work it out." We committed to doing whatever it took to make the marriage successful—to keep track of how well it was working and to find ways of overcoming obstacles.

As the marriage analogy implies, committing to any purpose is not to be taken lightly. It is a promise you make to yourself and to others that involves some personal accountability: you will be unhappy with yourself if you fail to deliver. People grieve when forced to abandon a commitment—it's like suffering a small death. Taking on a new commitment also involves investing a significant chunk of psychological energy in a task purpose. It is possible to become overcommitted—to feel too thinly stretched to function. At those times, you need to complete some of your tasks or get them back on track before you can find the energy to take on new ones.

Nevertheless, commitment is what we all need if we are to be effective in accomplishing the purposes we care about in an era of increasing uncertainties. General Gordon Sullivan, former Army Chief of Staff, put it well in the title of his recent book with Michael Harper: *Hope Is Not a Method*.[5]

Choosing Activities to Accomplish the Purpose

After committing to a purpose, the second event in self-management is deciding how to make the purpose happen—selecting activities that will accomplish it. Notice that commitment depends on this ability to choose, and vice versa. Without the freedom to choose proper activities, it would be pointless to commit to a purpose—to take personal responsibility for achieving it. You could not steer your behavior toward the purpose. You could only carry out prescribed activities as well as possible and hope that they would achieve the purpose. Likewise, without a committed purpose to steer it, choice becomes choice for its own sake, and degrades into simple whim or impulse.

Allowing workers to choose useful activities is the main point of the decentralized decision making in the new work. Workers use their intelligence in problem solving to find ways of dealing with the uncertainties they encounter: what would be a good way of achieving the task purpose given the circumstances they find? In self-management, workers tailor their work activities to the needs of the situation in ways that fixed rules cannot anticipate. Workers select appropriate work procedures and adapt or improve old procedures—or invent new ones—depending on the changing requirements of the task.

Choice involves freedom of thought—being able to act out of one's own understanding of the situation. The elaborate rules of the compliance era were intended to box in workers' judgment and behavior. I once saw a safety poster that actually said "DON'T THINK!"—implying that free thought was dangerous. In contrast, managers in the new work world are encouraging workers to think "outside the box." This "box" is made up of the old constraints on thinking: the elaborate rules, the established procedures and precedents, the tradition of relying on the boss's judgment rather than their own and of using prevailing assumptions instead of their own understanding. The freedom of thought of committed workers has become a vital competitive resource that produces inventions, innovations, continuous improvement, and renewal.

Monitoring for Competence

After choosing our activities, we begin to perform them. As we do so, the next event in self-management comes into play—monitoring our performance for competence. This event, then, involves making sure that our work activities meet our standards.

During the compliance era, work standards were external and set by managers at fixed levels. Workers were charged with doing work that met these levels—doing "good enough" or "satisfactory" work. In contrast, self-management involves committed workers' meeting their own internal standards of competence. Internal standards are more dynamic: people raise their standards on tasks they care about as they become more skilled and experienced at the task activities. Worker self-monitoring, then, can be a powerful force for improving performance.

The nature of the standards involved in self-monitoring depends on the type of activity involved. For a machinist, standards involve such things as the measurement specifications of a part, its finish, and the absence of any burrs. For a salesperson making a presentation to a group, the standards would be quite different: keeping the group's interest, conveying essential information, listening, answering questions, and remaining courteous. Standards generally cover aspects of activities that play a significant role in achieving the task purpose. Most of these standards are technical standards—standards relating to technique—but ethical standards may also be involved. The notion of worker *professionalism* includes both.

Regardless of the nature of the standards, the essential requirements of monitoring for competence are the same. People must pay attention to how well their standards are being met—be fully present, involved, focusing, concentrating on the task. They must also be prepared to make adjustments in their performance of the activity when threats and opportunities (uncertainties) arise. The machinist changes a machine setting and spends more time polishing a part as necessary; the salesperson rephrases a statement and provides another example in response to a customer question. Some of these adjustments may involve stopping to think, but with experience much of the adjustment becomes intuitive. As workers become more adept at the task, the activities and adjustments often blend more smoothly into a seamless and graceful flow.

Monitoring for Progress

The last event in the self-management process involves checking to see that the activities are actually accomplishing the purpose—that progress is being made. Like monitoring for competence of performance, this step involves an assessment of how the task is going, together with a willingness to take action to make changes. In contrast to monitoring competence, however, monitoring progress is a purpose-centered evaluation of how well the task is going.

I find that people sometimes miss this distinction, so I'll elaborate a bit. There are two parts to evaluating how the task is going—how well you are performing the activities (competence of performance) and how well the activities are accomplishing the task purpose (progress toward the purpose). Both are important. If you have chosen the right activities, the competence of your performance is likely to advance the purpose. In an uncertain world, however, you can't be sure that those activities are the right ones. So you have to keep checking to make sure that the purpose is being achieved. This is, after all, the bottom line of the task. Without monitoring for progress, you are only hoping that the task is on track.

Since most purposes involve helping an internal or external customer, monitoring task progress usually involves some form of customer feedback. On longer tasks, this means checking with the customer at different milestones and making any needed adjustments. The gardener, for example, checks with the customer at key points in the planning and planting of a garden. On shorter, more repetitive tasks, monitoring means checking with customers after they receive a product or service, and using that information to improve task activities to increase customer satisfaction in the future. The machinist learns whether the finished part works for a customer, and the salesperson finds out whether the customer makes a purchase. This use of customer feedback has become a cornerstone of much of the quality movement.

Measuring progress and collecting feedback from customers takes a certain amount of discipline. It takes time and energy away from performing task activities. There is also some psychological cost to reexamining your choices, exposing them to customer evaluation, and possibly having to make changes in your activities. But it's the only way for a committed worker to be sure the purpose is being achieved. Again, it's dramatic to contrast this aspect of self-management with the conventional wisdom of the compliance era, which concluded that "workers resist change." Looking back, the truth was more that, under command-and-control management, workers often resisted imposed change. In the new work, committed workers initiate changes when their purpose is threatened or they see a better way of accomplishing it.

Feedback and Learning

Finally, consider the rather innocent-looking feedback arrows in Figure 5.1. In reality, these arrows represent much of the value added of human intelligence in dealing with task uncertainties.

Feedback comes from the two monitoring events—monitoring for competence of performance and for progress toward the purpose. Think of this feedback as either positive or negative. When feedback is positive, it means that things are working as we expected—our efforts are resulting in competently performed activities and those activities are moving the purpose forward. Positive feedback strengthens our work habits and our assumptions about what works, as well as our commitment to the purpose. That's good, of course, but we could program machines to do all our work if these habits and assumptions always worked.

The real value of human intelligence shows up when the feedback is negative—when something isn't working. After all, that's how uncertainties show up in tasks: the expected doesn't happen. According to American educator John Dewey, that is also when learning is most likely to occur.[6] When things don't work, we look up to see what happened, try to figure out why, and come to a new understanding that is usually more complex than what we believed before. The new understanding leads to a new activity or adjustment. If that works, our new understanding is strengthened—until we encounter a new uncertainty and the learning cycle repeats itself. If something doesn't work, we keep trying to figure it out until we find something that works. If nothing works after a great deal of effort and experimentation, our commitment eventually declines, and—sadder but wiser—we move on to a new purpose.

Not only does this feedback produce more responsive and adaptive behavior, then, it also produces important forms of learning. As the work world has become more uncertain, organizations have realized the competitive value of this learning as a kind of intellectual capital, and have recognized the importance of becoming a "learning organization," to use Peter Senge's phrase.[7] It has become clearer that workers' learnings in the new work increase their value as human resources and make them more difficult to replace. It has also become clear that organizations need to invest resources in trying to capture or "harvest" this learning and share it with others in the organization who would find it helpful. Some of the learning is in the form of preconscious intuition and the physical artistry of a craftsman. But other learnings are more easily transferable. Some take the form of "lessons learned"—insights or theories that can be told to others. Others are specific innovations or inventions that can be used by others— new techniques or procedures, or new physical equipment.

What Happens to Managerial Control?

Notice that the self-management events in Figure 5.1 substitute for the traditional command-and-control activities performed by managers—deciding on a task purpose, assigning task activities to workers, supervising or directing those work activities to ensure they are done properly, and making sure that the purpose gets achieved. Many leaders who were used to command-and-control, then, have felt like they were losing control when their organization shifted to worker self-management. In reality, the shift represents a change of form for managerial control, rather than a loss of it. More of the nuts-and-bolts decision making is taken on by workers, but leaders stay informed on issues of performance competence and progress.

Under worker self-management, leaders also keep influencing workers, although the form of that influence shifts. The leader uses less authority and coercion to impose decisions, and provides more information and expert advice as inputs to workers' decision making. Several writers have used the metaphor of *partnership* to describe this relationship, underscoring the free flow of information between leader and team member as partners in the task purpose. A number of management writers have also used the metaphor of *coaching* to describe this new relationship.[8] As workers take responsibility for task purposes, they are more likely to welcome this helpful input and to seek it out—in the way that athletes welcome help from a knowledgeable coach. Jack Welch, CEO of General Electric, uses the metaphor of *boundarylessness* to describe this flow of helpful information and the removal of traditional barriers that interfere with it.[9]

It's helpful for leaders to remember that the switch to worker self-management is occurring because it is a way to *increase control* over the uncertainties facing a work team. By allowing workers to make more decisions on task uncertainties they encounter, team leaders are better able to leverage their time to deal with larger uncertainties facing the team. They can attend to planning, watch for dangers and opportunities facing the team, deal with personnel issues, and make sure that nothing important falls through the cracks.

As a practical matter, it's also important to remember that leaders retain their command-and-control authority and can use it if needed. As Peter Block notes, self-managing workers have the right to disagree with their leader's suggestions, but the leader also retains "51 percent" of the votes in the final decision when there is disagreement on an important issue.[10] The challenge for the leader, of course, is to lead in such a way that this over-ruling occurs fairly rarely—or else self-management becomes a sham.

All this assumes that workers are ready for self-management. That brings up the subject of worker development.

Worker Development

In a paper with Susan Hocevar and Gail Thomas, I proposed that *development* simply means moving toward greater self-management.[11] Think about this for a moment. Isn't that what we look for as our children develop, and what we mean by maturity? We look for young people to increasingly commit to worthwhile purposes and accept responsibility for them, to make their own decisions consistent with those purposes, to apply standards to their behavior, and to be resourceful and persistent in pursuing their purposes. Those are the kinds of lessons we try to teach our children, and the way we judge how responsible a young person is becoming. As parents, this is also what guides us in deciding how much "self-management" to allow our children as they grow up.

In many ways, then, self-management is simply a way of describing the task capabilities of an adult human being. To be self-managing at work is to fully engage those adult capabilities in one's work tasks.

Still, workers don't always come to a task ready to be fully self-managing. Younger workers may still be learning general self-management skills. Some workers of any age may be hesitant to self-manage, particularly if they are emerging from command-and-control management. Even workers who are predisposed to be self-managing may need to ease into it on new tasks as they learn new skills and gain experience. Other workers start to self-manage, run into difficulties, and become discouraged.

The development of worker self-management, then, is an important issue for leaders in today's work world. It is also an important issue for workers themselves—the key to their effectiveness and satisfaction, their level of responsibility, and even their long-term employability.

This takes me to the central motivational issues of this book. What are the intrinsic rewards that reinforce self-management and the development of self-management skills? How can leaders and workers increase those rewards so that self-management flourishes?

PART III

The Intrinsic Rewards of the New Work

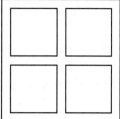

A Management Tale, concluded . . .

So once again the executives took their question to the new management gurus and consultants, saying, "How can we manage for Passion and Fulfillment? Vision is Not Enough."

"Ah, but you must Empower your people as well," said several gurus. So with great fanfare, many executives bade their managers delegate. Some workers rejoiced, but others were wary. And many managers led in their old ways. In time, people became cynical of empowerment, too, and saw this as another unkept promise.

"Pride and Professionalism are the key," said other gurus. So, again with much fanfare, executives commanded that their people be trained in issues of Character. And again the results were limited.

Soon the workers became weary of the new solutions and came to dread the fanfare that accompanied them. And yet the gurus found still more solutions. They counseled the executives to Measure all things, to provide much Training, to become Coaches, to Open their Ledgers, to make their business into a Learning Organization, to host Celebrations for their people, and still more.

In time, the executives came to realize that they could not embrace each new solution, for the solutions were too numerous, too unpredictable in their effects, and often too expensive. What they needed more than new solutions, they saw, was the Wisdom to tell which solutions would truly instill passion and fulfillment in their workers. For in truth they had been trying solutions without fully understanding the problem.

As they thought about this, the executives realized that there were basic facts they must learn about the elements of workers' passions for work, how to tell which were lacking, and how to provide conditions that would create those missing elements. And the study of Intrinsic Rewards was born.

6

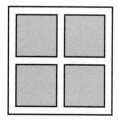

The Rewards of
Self-Management

The last episode of the "Management Tale" captures the piecemeal efforts to energize or inspire self-management in many of today's organizations. Consultants and writers have offered various recommendations based on important pieces of the puzzle of intrinsic motivation. Visions are an important part of inspiration, but not the whole. "Bureaucracy busting" and delegation provide necessary freedom, but are also not enough. Recently, training based on the work of leadership consultant Stephen Covey has been used to emphasize character-related issues of pride and professionalism.[1] Other writers emphasize celebrations, coaching, and customer feedback.

Each of these bits of advice contains valid but partial insights about intrinsic motivation. To be sure, each bit of advice can be useful. However, each one is likely to make a noticeable difference only if it provides the missing piece of motivation for a given group of workers. It can be unnecessary if that motivational piece is already in place, and will probably not be enough if more than one piece is missing. In this way, a number of potentially useful strategies are in danger of being overpromised and overused, which gradually results in cynicism. Clearly, there needs to be a more accurate way of diagnosing what's missing and understanding how to provide it.

This section of the book provides a diagnostic framework for intrinsic motivation. Chapter Six introduces the parts of the framework, beginning with a more complete map of the intrinsic rewards needed to reinforce

self-management. With this information, you can check to see what rewards are missing for team members and better direct motivational efforts
where they are needed. The second part of the framework is a set of building
blocks that are needed to produce each intrinsic reward. With this information, you can more precisely decide how to enhance an intrinsic reward by
checking to see which specific building blocks are missing. Chapters Seven
through Ten will discuss each intrinsic reward in more detail, along with
actions to provide the building blocks.

As you read the next four chapters, you will probably recognize many of
the action recommendations—most have already been publicized as alleged
solutions to the problems of the new work. The key value added of this section of the book, then, is not in recommending new solutions. Rather, it is
in providing a knowledge of intrinsic motivation and its requirements that
will help you choose actions that fit the needs of your particular situation.
Chances are that you'll learn a few new action tools, then, but the most important thing will be to learn when each tool can help and why.

First, the intrinsic rewards. . . .

Four Intrinsic Rewards

The four intrinsic rewards that energize the new work come directly from
the four main self-management events discussed in Chapter Five. Each of
those events requires the worker to make a judgment—of the meaningfulness of the task purpose, the degree of choice available in selecting activities, the competence with which those activities are performed, and the
amount of progress being made toward the task purpose.[2] These four judgments, then, are logical requirements of self-management. But they are
much more than that. They are not detached, arms-length judgments—
they carry a strong emotional charge. These emotional charges are the intrinsic rewards of self-management—the emotional "juices" that energize
and reinforce continued self-management. People feel good or excited about
a task—whether it produces a quiet glow of satisfaction or an exuberant
celebration—because of these judgments.

Try that idea on for a while. When you feel particularly good about
your work, doesn't it have something to do with realizing you're doing
something worthwhile (meaningfulness), being able to do something the

way you think it should be done (choice), performing some activity particularly well (competence), or making some significant advance toward accomplishing your purpose (progress)?

Walt Tymon and I have found it helpful to refer to these emotional charges, or feelings, as a *"sense* of meaningfulness," *"sense* of choice," and so on.[3] Figure 6.1 shows a way of grouping these four intrinsic rewards.

As shown by the rows, the sense of meaningfulness and the sense of progress come from the task purpose, while the sense of choice and the sense of competence come from the task activities. As shown by the columns, the senses of choice and of meaningfulness are feelings of task opportunity— being able to use your judgment and pursue a worthwhile purpose, respectively—and come from the early steps of the self-management process. They convey the idea that this is a good task to be engaged in—that performing these activities and pursuing this purpose are what one wants to

FIGURE 6.1 The Four Intrinsic Rewards

	OPPORTUNITY Rewards	**ACCOMPLISHMENT** Rewards
From Task **ACTIVITIES**	Sense of **CHOICE**	Sense of **COMPETENCE**
From Task **PURPOSE**	Sense of **MEANINGFULNESS**	Sense of **PROGRESS**

Source: Modified and reproduced by special permission of the Publisher, Consulting Psychologists Press, Inc., Palo Alto, CA 94303 from *Empowerment Inventory* by Kenneth W. Thomas and Walter G. Tymon, Jr. Copyright 1983 by Xicom, Incorporated. All rights reserved. Duplication in whole or part prohibited. Xicom, Incorporated is a subsidiary of Consulting Psychologists Press, Inc.

be doing. The senses of competence and of progress, on the other hand, are feelings of accomplishment related to the performance of activities and attainment of the purpose, respectively. These two rewards come from the monitoring steps that occur later in the self-management process. Together, they provide the idea that the task is going well. (For information on how these four rewards build on earlier models of intrinsic motivation, see Appendix A.)

Here are brief descriptions of the four intrinsic rewards, in the order they occur during the self-management process. They are adapted from the *Empowerment Inventory* that Walt Tymon and I developed to measure them:[4]

- A sense of *meaningfulness* is the opportunity you feel to pursue a worthy task purpose. The feeling of meaningfulness is the feeling that you are on a path that is worth your time and energy—that you are on a valuable mission, that your purpose matters in the larger scheme of things.
- A sense of *choice* is the opportunity you feel to select task activities that make sense to you and to perform them in ways that seem appropriate. The feeling of choice is the feeling of being free to choose—of being able to use your own judgment and act out of your own understanding of the task.
- A sense of *competence* is the accomplishment you feel in skillfully performing task activities you have chosen. The feeling of competence involves the sense that you are doing good, high-quality work on a task.
- A sense of *progress* is the accomplishment you feel in achieving the task purpose. The feeling of progress involves the sense that the task is moving forward, that your activities are really accomplishing something.

How These Intrinsic Rewards Work

Figure 6.2 shows how the intrinsic rewards are linked to self-management.[5] Both make up an ongoing system of mutual influence—a sort of dance in which either can take the lead. The self-management events on the right provide the judgments that produce the intrinsic rewards on the left. Those intrinsic rewards, in turn, energize (reinforce) continued self-management, which provides updated judgments, and so on.

FIGURE 6.2 A Self-Reinforcing Cycle

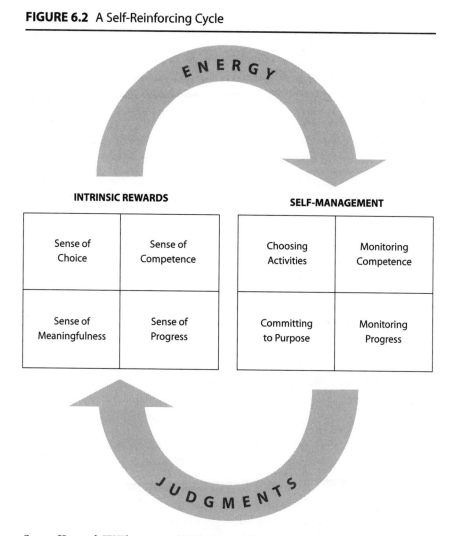

Source: Kenneth W. Thomas and Erik Jansen, "Intrinsic Motivation in the Military: Models and Strategic Importance," Technical Report NPS-SM-96-001, Monterey, CA: Naval Postgraduate School, September 1996.

This kind of system can produce upward or downward spirals. A change in either self-management or intrinsic rewards can cause this kind of shift. For example, if you interfere with some part of workers' self-management, you will tend to reduce their intrinsic rewards, which will provide less energy for self-management, further reducing intrinsic rewards, and so on. Likewise, if you increase a worker's intrinsic rewards, you will tend to energize more self-management, which will probably lead to further increases in intrinsic rewards, and so on, until some new, higher equilibrium is reached.

In this system, then, the intrinsic rewards provide important leverage. They can bring about an increase in self-management, with its greater commitment, innovation, and other benefits. As discussed earlier, the intrinsic rewards also produce benefits of increased job satisfaction and worker retention. The research done so far on this new model of intrinsic motivation supports these benefits. Since Betty Velthouse and I first proposed the model in 1990, I've done some studies with my colleague Walt Tymon from Villanova University, and much good work has also been done by Gretchen Spreitzer at USC, as well as others. (See the chapter notes for references.[6]) So far, these studies show that the intrinsic rewards are consistently related to job satisfaction and to performance. These findings hold across types of organizations and for managers as well as workers. Studies have also shown that the intrinsic rewards are related to innovativeness, commitment to the organization, and reduced stress.

A Positive Role for Leaders

What can leaders do to shift this system of self-management and intrinsic rewards upward? In other words, what does this model tell us about the leader's role in motivating and developing workers?

In his later years, quality advocate W. Edwards Deming emphasized intrinsic motivation, which he often referred to as "pride of workmanship" or "joy in work."[7] However, his writings emphasized what leaders commonly did wrong that stifled intrinsic motivation. Most of his motivational advice, then, was about what *not* to do—for example, not managing by fear, quotas, or inappropriate reward systems. Some of the building blocks in the following chapters deal with the points Deming covered, but I have tried to recast them in terms of a more positive role. Rather than focusing on not pushing the system downward, it seems more useful to think of the leader's role as finding ways to keep pushing it upward—to get beyond not being a negative influence and work at being a continuous positive influence.

Figure 6.3 provides a shorthand way of thinking about this positive leadership role. It's based on feedback I gave to an organization that was having trouble developing self-management in many of its work teams. This particular organization used the "coaching" metaphor, so I tried to expand on that idea. "Coaching" was a little too vague to capture the key elements of leadership that were needed. At its core, coaching has to do with helping players build their skill or competence of performance. This is an important part of the leadership role, as the figure shows. But in reality good coaches, like other good leaders, do much more to develop players. So I used three more sports terms to draw attention to other parts of leadership that were often neglected in this organization. Some supervisors acting as coaches were micromanagers who continued to use command-and-control, so I pointed out that "handing off" is what allows workers to develop choice. Good coaches also have a tradition of inspiring people—building meaningfulness by focusing attention on an important purpose. Finally, good coaches keep players energized and developing by scorekeeping on measures of progress and by cheering or celebrating that progress when it occurs. *Coaching* on its own addresses only the competence aspect of work, but taken together with *handing off, inspiring,* and *scorekeeping and cheering* it provides a pretty good overview of the positive leadership that can help you develop and motivate workers.

FIGURE 6.3 The Role of Leadership

Leading for CHOICE: **HANDING OFF**	Leading for COMPETENCE: **COACHING**
Leading for MEANINGFULNESS: **INSPIRING**	Leading for PROGRESS: **SCOREKEEPING and CHEERING**

To decide which of these aspects of leadership has the highest priority in a situation, leaders will need to take stock of the levels of the four intrinsic rewards in their team—to locate the greatest motivational needs (and opportunities). This can be done pretty well by talking honestly with team members about these intrinsic rewards. To get a more precise reading, or to track improvements over time, the *Empowerment Inventory* that Walt Tymon and I designed is also available through Consulting Psychologists Press.[8] Using either method, leaders will want to get a fix on which intrinsic rewards are strongest and which are relatively weak and need attention. In a medical facility, for example, I've found that meaningfulness is usually very high, since lives are at stake, but the other rewards often need more help.

Building Blocks for the Intrinsic Rewards

This gets me to the second part of the diagnostic framework—the *building blocks* of each reward. These are the set of conditions that allow each reward to flourish. Figure 6.4 lists the sets of building blocks that Walt Tymon and I culled from our research and experience, and from the management literature.[9] Each set of building blocks serves as a checklist to troubleshoot any missing conditions that need attention for that intrinsic reward—to identify why an intrinsic reward is low and what needs to be provided.

The next four chapters will discuss these building blocks in detail, along with specific actions that can be taken to provide them. At this point, however, I want to emphasize two things about these building blocks and actions.

It Takes More Than Job Design

One of the classic models of intrinsic motivation, by Richard Hackman and Greg Oldham, focused exclusively on aspects of job design as influences on intrinsic motivation.[10] (Their model is briefly described in Appendix A.) A number of the building blocks in Figure 6.4 involve these kinds of job design factors—fairly objective things that can be engineered into jobs, like authority, information sources, whole tasks, and measurement

FIGURE 6.4 Building Blocks for the Intrinsic Rewards

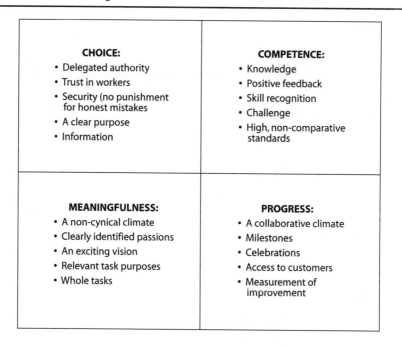

and feedback mechanisms. They enable self-management to occur and to be effective. They continue to be very important, but they are not enough!

Since that model was developed in the 1960s, there has been a profound change in the social sciences. In this postmodern era, it is now more obvious that there is only a loose connection between so-called objective events and our reactions to them. There are basic ambiguities in many events that allow them to be interpreted in various ways. Human behavior, we realize now, is shaped more directly by our interpretation of those events than by the events themselves.[11] So we pay a great deal more attention now to how people interpret events—to how they "frame" events and "construct" their meaning. For example, it is clear that transformational or inspirational leaders are effective because they actively shape people's interpretations of the task purpose.[12]

For that reason, a number of the building blocks in Figure 6.4 involve things that shape workers' interpretations in rewarding ways—that make tasks more fulfilling. These kinds of building blocks are especially important to a sense of meaningfulness. For example, it is important for leaders to help workers avoid cynical interpretations of the task purpose, and to create a vision of a desirable future that appeals to their passions. But interpretive factors show up in the building blocks of the other intrinsic rewards as well. Judgments of progress depend on identifying milestones, for example, and celebrations are ways of drawing attention to that progress. These interpretive factors, then, enhance or *amplify* the intrinsic rewards that workers get from self-management, providing an added motivational boost to their self-management.

Workers Shape These Building Blocks, Too

When I started doing research on intrinsic motivation, most management writers seemed to assume that empowerment was something you did *to* workers. That seemed a little ironic, since the whole point of empowerment was greater self-management and proactivity for workers. Looking back, that assumption was probably a remnant of the paternalism of the compliance era.

The reality is that workers in the new work world play an increasingly active role in co-determining the building blocks in Figure 6.4. They share information and propose their own interpretations of events. They negotiate with leaders and their teammates to initiate changes in their job designs. They are influenced by leaders, but also, in Charles Manz's phrase, exercise "self-leadership" in many ways.[13] This co-determining of the building blocks occurs between team leaders and team members all up and down the hierarchy.

For that reason, the next four chapters will describe actions to help create the building blocks from two perspectives. The first will involve what leaders can do to help construct the building blocks for their team members. The second involves what individuals can do to help shape the building blocks for their own jobs.

7

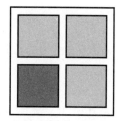

Building a Sense
of Meaningfulness

You know a task is meaningful to you when you find yourself excited about the task. It's easy to concentrate on the task—to focus your attention and energy on it. In fact, you are likely to find yourself resenting the time you spend on other, less meaningful tasks and to borrow time from those tasks so that you can devote more time to the one that matters. You find yourself thinking about the task a great deal, and your subconscious works on the task even when you are not consciously thinking about it, so that you come back to the task with new insights. You find that you are judging how productive a day you had by whether or not you were able to make progress on this task, rather than getting sucked in by other demands on your time. You also see clear signs of your own commitment to the task in how you manage to find ways around obstacles and how you don't take no for an answer.

When a task is not meaningful to you, in contrast, you have little emotional investment in it. You feel relatively detached and unrelated to what's going on with the task. The task is empty for you. It's as though you are waiting for something else more significant to come along and are marking time or making do until it does. If you have other, more meaningful tasks to work on, then it is likely that you resent the time you spend on this less meaningful task. You are likely to find yourself avoiding or delaying working on this task, and to find that you are easily distracted while working on it. You may have to force yourself to keep working on the task, so that your thinking goes something like this: "OK, suck it up. You *have* to do this." If you hit a roadblock or encounter a no from a superior, it is easy (and even a relief) to drop the task.

Understanding Meaningfulness

I used to say that meaningful purposes were the ones that fit people's values. But meaningfulness is about the energy attached to a purpose, and *values* seems too dry a word to capture that. The word *passion* conveys that sense of energy better, as in "a passion for—." Meaningfulness, then, is about the passion you have for a task purpose.

People's passions tend to develop and change over their work lives.[1] Younger workers are deeply involved in learning the ropes about their work (and about life in general). So at that stage of life, their passions at work often involve showing that they can handle things. The phrases that describe these passions convey the sense that they are being tested and have something to prove: being able to "cut the mustard," "find their sea legs," "stand on their own two feet," "make a go of it," "earn their keep," or "make the grade."

But as workers begin to complete this stage and to realize that they *can* do the work, their passions tend to shift. There is a common "crisis of meaning" at this point, and they begin to need more from their work and lives. The work often feels empty, and workers find that they need to answer a new set of questions: "OK, I can do the work. Now, do I want to? Why?" In struggling with these questions, workers begin to discover their particular areas of passion for work, finding those purposes that have meaning for them and sustain them emotionally.

There is a fair amount of diversity in people's passions, in part because they are influenced by personal history. For example, I had two otherwise loving parents who were not very good at listening. I find now that I have a passion for communicating ideas, which fires me up in the classroom and is sustaining me through the writing of this book. My friends, with different histories, find great meaning in other types of purposes: fighting injustice, making beautiful things, pushing technological advances, getting teams to pull together, or making useful things with their hands. In any organization, this diversity of passion means that it is important to match individuals with the tasks that have meaning for them. This means getting to know people's passions, making judicious task assignments, and asking for volunteers when possible—to allow workers to do their own matching of passions to tasks.[2]

However, there is also a considerable amount of commonality of passion within most work groups—not totally, but enough to make it possible for groups to be energized by a shared, meaningful purpose. Some of this commonality comes from workers' self-selecting into fields of work that match their passions, and some comes from shared work history in the group. For example, some work groups will have a shared passion to develop a new product they believe in, or to develop a report that "knocks people's socks off."

Finally, there are also shared passions that cut across individuals and organizations. The deepest of these are *spiritual* passions. I am not necessarily talking about spiritual in the sense of organized religion here, although religions speak directly to these passions. Rather, I am talking about a deeply felt desire to have one's life make a difference in the larger scheme of things, to make a contribution, to lead a worthy life that one can be proud of, to be "on the right path."[3] As noted earlier, these passions often show up in terms of being of service to customers and of bettering society or people's lives in some way. In my case, then, my passion for communicating ideas has merged with a desire to help people: my deepest satisfaction in work is to give people insights that help their lives work better.

I invite you to stop for a minute to think about your own passions. What gets you excited at work? What touches you deeply?

Leading for Meaningfulness

The rest of this chapter deals with the practical issue of how to build a sense of meaningfulness. The material is organized around five building blocks of meaningfulness:

- Non-cynical climate
- Clearly identified passions
- Exciting vision
- Relevant task purposes
- Whole tasks

Each of these building blocks, when missing, is an obstacle to meaningfulness. So this set of building blocks can be used as a diagnostic tool to troubleshoot low meaningfulness. I will cover actions to help create each building block when it is missing, tackling the problem from two points of view. This section discusses what leaders can do to help craft these building blocks for workers on their teams. The following section will cover what individuals can do for their own jobs.

A brief note here about writing style. . . . This book is likely to be read by different audiences—leaders, workers, human resource managers, consultants, trainers, and academics. For impact, I have written this section and the next as though I am speaking directly to the leader or job holder. I ask your patience if that's not the case. But I also encourage you to try on this material at a personal level. After all, we are all job holders (even those who are self-employed) and most of us exercise leadership roles in different settings.

Building a Non-Cynical Climate

Some people get their kicks stompin' on a dream. . . .
—SINATRA[4]

It is very difficult for a work group to get energized around a meaningful purpose if the members don't feel safe to talk about their passions. One of the greatest joys of group work is a shared excitement about what is possible. But one or two vocal cynics can be enough to stifle the excitement.

Consider what cynicism is about. Cynical comments are aimed at embarrassing or shaming people who express idealism and passion. So, instead of workers' being energized and rewarded by their passions, cynicism serves to punish and suppress those passions—the opposite of what you want to happen. So it is important that the leader counter these voices in group discussions and help to establish group norms that encourage idealism and passion.

How do you do that? Peter Block spells it out well in his book *Stewardship*.[5] The power of cynics, according to Block, is that they have facts to support their position. There *have* been idealistic purposes that didn't pan out in the past, and passions that were disappointed. So it doesn't make sense to argue that the cynics are wrong. You can acknowledge those past disappointments and empathize with them. But you also need to point out that cynicism and passion are choices that people make. You can announce your own decision to strive to accomplish something of value. And you can invite others to join you, including the cynics. Once the remainder of the group see the choice, it will be hard for them to say, "Yes, cynicism is a great choice; let's work without hope and passion."

Clearly Identifying Passions

There is a longing in each of us to invest in things that matter.
—PETER BLOCK[6]

The team needs to identify its shared passions for a number of reasons. Identifying passions moves them (and the associated intrinsic rewards) to the foreground in the team's thinking about motivation. Otherwise, team members may be thinking they are mostly there for the money, although most will recognize that the work is sometimes fulfilling. You can remind people that all the team members could be doing other things to earn a living, but have chosen to do this work. What is it that team members care about? Without the clarity created by identifying and naming passions, a sense of meaningfulness is a mysterious, hit-or-miss experience at work. Once the team understands the contents of its passions, it can pursue meaningfulness in a more systematic way: "Aha, that's what we care about. Now let's go after it." Finally, understanding its shared passions is a powerful unifying force for a team. Teammates are likely to think more highly of each other and to treat each other as allies in pursuit of a common purpose.

Note that this building block is not about getting the team to endorse any top-down mission statement. Nor is it about trying to sell your own passions to the rest of the team. If you are to harness the passions of the team, you want to start by learning what those passions are. So you will need to talk with your team members, one on one, about what they care most deeply about in the work. As you do this, you will probably find that some workers won't be able to answer very directly. Some younger workers may just be discovering that they have passions for their work, and others will know that they have passions but won't be able to label them very well. But most will be able to give you examples of times when they have been most excited or cared most about their work. Here, you can suggest words that help them pinpoint their passions until you both get a handle on them.

As you have these conversations, you are likely to find that many workers have settled for work that does not fulfill their passions because they haven't believed that fulfilling work is possible. To get at their passions, you might talk with them about their *dreams*. Dreams are not low-level, practical, or compromised purposes. They are more audacious, and more directly related to passions. You will be able to feel the difference in tone, energy level, and even posture when people's conversation gets into the vicinity of their passions and dreams. It is a powerful reminder of the energy and potential fulfillment involved.

After you have talked with your team members, you can identify the largest areas of overlap in the team's passions. I suggest you share your findings with the group as a whole to get their reactions. But be aware that once this happens and the group begins to talk openly about its passions, group members will want some significant action to pursue those passions. You and the team will need to follow through in some significant way, or you will be creating more cynicism.

Providing an Exciting Vision

If you don't know what the end result is supposed to look like, you can't get there.
—VINCE LOMBARDI[7]

Big, hairy, audacious goals.
—JAMES COLLINS AND JERRY PORRAS[8]

A vision is a big purpose for the team—a macro image of a future that the team wants to create. It crystallizes the team's passions into an audacious and exciting possibility that captures the team's imagination. It is a shared, realizable dream that team members can harness their efforts to achieve. Without this shared vision, the team's passions lack a focus or target and can be dissipated in different, uncoordinated directions.

As leader, you can get lots of input from the team for this vision. But stating the vision and backing it up are ultimately your responsibility. Leadership researchers James Kouzes and Barry Posner found that teams' strongest needs from their leaders were a vision for the team and personal integrity in its pursuit.[9] Note that developing a vision is not a one-time, check-the-box requirement. Leaders need to keep stating the vision and backing it up with action.

What does a good vision look like? It must speak to the team's shared passions. In a technical service unit within an organization, for example, shared passions may involve cutting-edge technological innovation and helping clients. A good vision statement for that unit might involve becoming a *recognized leader in technical innovation* with *delighted clients*. But such a simple statement is not enough. A more complete and concrete picture needs to be painted of what this would look like. For example: the team would hold a number of patents, be benchmarked by similar units in other organizations, and be invited to professional conferences to speak on its innovations. Likewise, the team would get high satisfaction ratings from its clients, receive many referrals from current clients, and receive many unsolicited testimonials for its work. These details make the vision more real and compelling for team members. Equally important, they will later provide ways of recognizing progress toward attaining the vision.

Ensuring Relevant Task Purposes

I want to get to a point where people challenge their bosses every day. Why do you require me to do these wasteful things?
—JACK WELCH[10]

While a vision is a big purpose for the team, team members' day-to-day work is made up of smaller, more concrete tasks—making things, ordering supplies, filling out reports, attending meetings, and so on. It isn't enough to have an exciting vision if many of these micro work tasks remain mundane or pointless. To energize one's work, it is important that these day-to-day tasks clearly contribute to the vision. Otherwise the drag of the mundane tasks saps the energy provided by the relevant ones.

The team's vision, then, provides a rationale for redesigning and pruning the tasks performed by team members. Busywork tasks that do not clearly contribute (often called "B.S." by workers) need to be eliminated.

Necessary housekeeping tasks with little value added for the vision can be subcontracted where possible, or at least simplified. The goal is to free more time to devote to realizing the vision. Part of your job as leader is to buffer the team from low-return demands. Among other things, this means negotiating with superiors and other departments to reduce paperwork requirements—and making sure that you call meetings only for important issues and run them efficiently.

Enlist your team members to play a major role in this work redesign. The excitement of the vision can provide the necessary energy. In the last few years, General Electric has had great successes in bottom-up redesign through its "Workout" process.[11] I have seen the energy and creativity that emerges from this process when people realize that their bosses will actually listen to their recommendations for eliminating pointless procedures. This can happen in your group. Redesign doesn't have to be imposed on workers. If workers are committed to a meaningful purpose, they will initiate changes to remove obstacles to its accomplishment.

Providing Whole Tasks

> *Completion of a whole and identifiable piece of work. . . .*
> *It is more meaningful to assemble a complete toaster than*
> *to solder electrical connections on toaster after toaster.*
> —J. Richard Hackman and Greg Oldham[12]

Finally, it is important that work tasks be designed or allocated so that individual workers are given whole projects where possible, or at least major, identifiable portions of a project. This established principle of job design allows workers to make a larger, more identifiable contribution. It also provides workers a larger potential source of pride. In thinking about this building block, I find it useful to imagine workers bringing their children to work and trying to answer the question, "What do you do?" If the answer is a long list of miscellaneous little tasks, it is hard to imagine the children (or their parent) feeling much pride. So it is helpful to give service workers responsibility for all services required by a given set of clients, and to give a staff member responsibility for an entire report (rather than collecting data for some of it).

Building Meaningfulness for Yourself

There's a lot you can do to build a sense of meaningfulness in your own job. Some of these actions involve negotiating with your boss. As you read through this section, keep in mind that these are the same basic actions that the workers you lead can take to increase their sense of meaningfulness. So try to be as receptive to their actions as you would like your own boss to be.

Creating a Non-Cynical Climate for Yourself

> *What is a cynic? A man who knows the price of everything,*
> *and the value of nothing.*
> —OSCAR WILDE[13]

For starters, it will be important for you to control any cynicism you may have. This will be vital to your own success as a leader, but also to your own intrinsic motivation at work. How do you do that? I've done research with Walt Tymon on thinking habits that influence intrinsic motivation.[14] We learned that people's thoughts are shaped by the implicit questions they ask themselves. If you size up situations by first asking yourself what's wrong, for example, you will nearly always find something that is wrong or could go wrong—and your perceptions of the world around you will be heavy in deficiencies and problems. We called this habit "deficiency focusing," and found that people who use it tend to get fewer intrinsic rewards from their work and to experience more stress.[15] This kind of thinking is a habit that can be changed. If you find that you do this, you can begin to balance your approach to situations by stopping to ask yourself what is going well and can go well. The goal here isn't to ignore problems but rather to get a more balanced view that doesn't put problems in center stage. Basically, you have to realize that this is a choice, and keep choosing to see a more balanced view that includes more positives—a view that encourages hope and passion.[16]

In addition, it is also important to seek out the company of non-cynical people who will help nurture your passions and ideals. This is something to look for in choosing a mentor and in picking friends and allies from among your peer group. You want people who will help you see opportunities, not those who will say, "Isn't that the pits—so typical around here."

Clarifying Your Own Passions

> *Discover what moves you.*
> —RICHARD LEIDER[17]

A few pages back, I invited you to think about your own passions. If a clear picture did not emerge, you have some work to do. This will be an important investment in the quality of your work life, so take some time to figure it out. It will be impossible to go after what fulfills you if you don't know what it is. Think about the times you have felt excited and fulfilled at work. What do they have in common? What dreams do you have about your ideal work? If possible, talk with supportive people in your life about this, to get a clearer picture of your passions. There are also a number of useful books that you can draw on for help. (See the chapter notes.[18])

Once you have a clear understanding of your passions, don't keep them a secret. Share this information with your boss and people in your peer team. That way, they can help funnel "your kind" of projects or assignments to you.

One final comment here. Some people are hesitant to examine their passions and dreams because they suspect that they don't fit their current job or organization. My philosophy is that it's better to find that out now and to act on it, rather than staying in the job and "rusting out," to use Richard Leider's phrase.[19] You won't be doing anyone a favor in the long run—yourself, your family and friends, or your coworkers—if you stay in a job that saps your energies. Find a team that shares your passions!

Crafting Your Own Vision

> *The vision needs to be lofty in order to capture our imagination and engage our spirit.*
> —PETER BLOCK[20]

You need to be daring here if you want to tap your passions. Crafting a personal vision isn't the kind of short-term goal-setting that encourages you to take small, obviously possible steps from where you are now. This is more about taking a longer leap into an inspiring future. What would you like your work to be like? What would deeply fulfill you or give you joy?

If this vision isn't daring, it isn't likely to make much of a difference in your life. If it is daring, the excitement of that future possibility will begin to pull you forward, and you will begin finding ways to make it happen. What kind of tasks do you want to be working on? What do you want to be accomplishing, and for whom? How will you recognize it when it is happening? What will your relationships with teammates look like?

Your personal vision will set an important example for team members when you begin to help your team develop its vision, and your personal vision can provide a nucleus for the team's vision. So you will want to develop your personal vision—at least in rough draft form—before you begin to talk about a vision for the team. In the same way, your personal and team visions can set an example for the higher-level peer team of which you are a member. Share these visions with your boss and peers. Serve as an advocate for a vision statement at that level that fits your personal and team visions.

Making Your Tasks More Relevant

The courage to say no . . . .
What's worth doing?
—RICHARD LEIDER[21]

I have found that I need to reinvent many of my work tasks to make them meaningful. I remember a turning point early in our research when Walt Tymon and I had to make a conference presentation but had low energy levels for it. We talked about how it was time to get on with the task, and we looked at the topic to see what we "had to" do. Then, after a pause, we looked at each other and said, "Wait a minute. What could we do that would be meaningful?" Our enthusiasm reappeared, and we planned a dynamite session that got across what we felt was an important message. Since then, I now routinely ask myself, or my colleagues, "What could I [or we] do here that is meaningful?" when approaching a new task. That question serves to get me back in touch with my passions and vision, and to identify what I want to accomplish. I invite you to use this same question.

Some tasks have little meaning, of course. As before, you'll want to negotiate to eliminate or simplify tasks with little value. And you'll want to initiate—or volunteer for—new tasks that better fit your passions and vision. When I can, I also ration the amount of time I spend on lower-value tasks, especially during my most creative time of the day. I find that if I start the day by working on the most meaningful tasks, I have enough energy to get through some of the less meaningful tasks in the afternoon—without the feeling that I have wasted the day. From the point of view of managing your energy, then, time management is not about doing everything more efficiently. Rather it is about making sure you spend your creative time on the tasks that are the most meaningful for you.

Negotiating for Whole Tasks

Doing a job from beginning to end with a visible outcome. . . .
—J. Richard Hackman and Greg Oldham[22]

The principle of assigning whole, identifiable tasks has been applied mostly to workers rather than managers. After all, it was workers who suffered the most job simplification during the compliance era, and the recent effort has been to improve their situation. Managers' jobs have always been relatively complex.

Still, there are times when the size or wholeness of a task is an issue for managers, either individually or for task forces on which they sit. It is more meaningful to deal with a whole problem, including its causes, than to address one small part of a remedy, for example. Likewise, it is more meaningful to recommend a solution and then oversee its implementation than to simply make the recommendation. If you are going to be involved in a project, it is worth trying to make it a meaningful whole—something that you can take pride in.

8

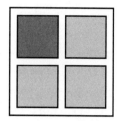

Building a Sense of Choice

You know you have a sense of choice on a task when you are aware that your views and insights matter—when you need to bring your understanding and judgment to the party. If you stopped to think about it, you would find that you feel very much like an adult in these situations—with the expansive feeling of being a responsible decision maker, driving your own train. You also find that you are absorbed in understanding the task: you are curious, interested—wanting to learn and open to information. You see visible signs of your choice in the flexibility of your behavior: you make adjustments and improvise as you see what would work better or as the situation changes. Your choices are also likely to show up in initiative, innovation and creativity, and experimentation. You also feel a strong sense of ownership of the task, and feel personally responsible for the outcomes of your decisions.

When you feel little sense of choice, in contrast, you feel constrained and pushed by other people and forces that are driving the train. You have the sense that your own views are irrelevant, so that you need to suppress them and comply. If you stopped to think about it, you would find that you don't feel much like an adult in these situations. You are likely to feel more like a younger child looking to adults or older siblings for direction. You are also likely to feel more pressure and to be more concerned about meeting others' expectations about how to do things correctly. Your lack of choice is visible in your need to more rigidly comply with procedures and directions, with little room for initiative or creativity. Finally, you are less likely to feel personally responsible for the task outcomes.

Understanding Choice

The experience of choice is connected to our early experiences with authority.[1] Children are dependent upon parents, older siblings, and other authority figures. On the whole (but with exceptions, as every parent knows), children learn to comply with the requests of those authorities. We learn that these authorities know more about many things and control resources that are important to us, and come to accept their right to make many decisions for us. In this position of dependency, we learn to be sensitive to authorities' desires, and we feel a pressure to satisfy them and to comply with their directions. Later, as teenagers, we commonly go through periods of *counterdependence* or rebellion. Here, we discover that our own judgments have value and that parents and other authorities are fallible. So we go through periods of looking for—and reacting against—any behavior by authority figures that appears arbitrary or unfair. Ideally, most of us get through that stage and reach a more adult sense of interdependence. In that state, we realize that we and authorities both have useful but imperfect insights and we work together to accomplish shared goals. We exchange information and views with managers, accept the need for them to make final decisions on some issues, and use our own judgment to carry out tasks over which we have some autonomy. Here, relations with managers have more of the quality of respect between adults, rather than parent-child paternalism and dependency.

With this background, it isn't hard to see why the experience of choice is emotionally loaded for us, and why a sense of choice is intrinsically rewarding. It's partly about feeling grown up. Chris Argyris began pointing out in the late 1950s that traditional management could stunt workers' development and keep them in a state of dependency.[2] Today, psychologists also show how being treated in paternalistic or controlling ways can make us relive childhood feelings.[3] We are likely to feel like children (small, dependent) or teenagers (resentful, rebellious) when we are told what to do and when our ideas are not listened to. In contrast, we feel more like adults when we exercise choice and are listened to. The notion of being able to make choices is so central to the experience of being an adult that a number of writers define the *self* as the part of us that chooses.[4] Exercising choice is fundamental to the way we attempt to control events in our lives. The psychologist DeCharms described the experience of choice as the feeling of being the "origin" of one's own behavior, in contrast to the feeling of being a "pawn" of external events and forces.[5] In a very real way, then, we lose our sense of self when we are not able to make choices—and we shut down emotionally and disengage from the task.

Choice takes on extra importance when we are committed to a meaningful purpose. Then a sense of choice means *being able to do what makes sense to you to accomplish the purpose.* It means being able to use your intelligence, take the best course of action, and make effective use of your time. In short, choice allows you to be performing those activities that you experience as useful. When you are not free to choose, on the other hand, you often find yourself doing things in ways that seem silly or a waste of time—with resulting frustration. It is impressive how much frustration you can tap in many committed people by asking them about the pointless rules or directives that interfere with their work.

Finally, a sense of choice also gives you a feeling of ownership of the task. When you make choices about how to perform a task, you redesign it to some degree and it becomes your own. You also feel personally responsible for task accomplishment—for the quality of your activities and the progress you make toward the purpose.[6] After all, if quality and progress result from *your* decisions, you deserve to feel proud of those accomplishments. The same is true for feeling responsible for low performance competence and a lack of progress. I find that few micromanagers seem to understand this. If a boss insists on making detailed decisions for workers and things go badly, it isn't surprising that workers feel less responsible for the outcome than the manager would like. It was the boss's decisions that produced the result, not their own; they had little control over events.

Leading for Choice

Of the four intrinsic rewards, leaders have the most control over workers' sense of choice. Leadership style is often described by the amount of choice given workers—from autocratic (little choice) to participative or delegative (much choice).[7] Likewise, advocates of job enrichment or worker empowerment have emphasized the importance of the leader's delegation of authority to workers. Still, this delegation is not always a simple matter. And delegating authority is only one step in creating a genuine sense of choice. There are five building blocks of choice:

- Delegated authority
- Trust in workers
- Security (no punishment for honest mistakes)
- Clear purpose
- Information

Delegating Authority

Power to act and make decisions about the work in all of its aspects.
—EDWARD LAWLER[8]

Delegation gives a worker the formal right (authority) to make decisions on a task within whatever limits are spelled out. Management books often make delegation sound like a clean, unilateral action by the leader. Actually, delegation is often a messy, interactive process, and is sometimes the result of workers' pressuring for more choice. It involves negotiations and discussions that need to take into account the workers' abilities to self-manage.

Here, I need to discuss the leadership trap of *micromanagement*—a trap that many well-intentioned leaders fall into. The mechanisms of the trap work something like this. You would like to delegate more authority to workers, and decide that you will do this as soon as the workers show they can handle it. In the meantime, you feel the need to closely manage and control events, making most of the operational decisions. What you are less aware of is that this micromanagement—even if you intend it to be temporary—often prevents the workers from being able to self-manage or otherwise show that they could handle more authority. So workers continue to act in a dependent way and you are trapped into an exhausting attempt to make all the decisions, while wondering why workers aren't as responsible as you are.

What's the way around this trap? I conducted a study with two colleagues, Susan Hocevar and Gail Fann Thomas, in an organization that had implemented worker self-management.[9] Where groups were having trouble becoming self-managing, sure enough, we found that leaders felt conflicted and stuck over being able to let go: they knew they were supposed to delegate, but didn't feel their teams were ready. In contrast, where workers had made the change more successfully, we found leaders who saw their job in terms of *developing* workers. Even though workers weren't fully ready, these managers committed to the development of self-management in their teams, and then began to delegate enough authority for them to grow into. These managers discussed delegation, team development, and self-management quite openly with the teams. They reached agreement on the team's current level of self-management, gave the team a manageable level of increased authority that took some stretching to cope with, helped team members develop the self-management skill to handle it, and then kept repeating these steps.

Demonstrating Trust

If you put fences around people, you get sheep.
Give people the room they need.
—JAMES COLLINS and JERRY PORRAS, citing a 3M phrase[10]

Once you delegate, it's important that you not hover nearby, waiting to grab the reins again if needed. I've spoken with leaders and teams that are caught in a yo-yo-like cycle of delegation, reclaimed authority, redelegation, and so on. Team members in this situation realize that the choices are not really theirs, and keep looking over their shoulder to see when the boss will step in. It's a matter of trust. To experience choice, the team needs to trust that you will keep your word and give them the room to make decisions, and you need to trust them enough to do so.

Trust also means removing unnecessary rules and controls that prevent team members from using their judgment. To do this, it is useful to shift the questions you ask yourself in evaluating rules and controls. Rather than asking the conservative question, "How do I know I should remove this rule [or control]?," a more appropriate question is, "Is there any obvious value added that prevents me from *eliminating* this rule [or control]?" General Electric, for example, has reduced unnecessary approvals by teaching the following principle: if you haven't made a significant number of rejections, stop requiring team members to get your approval.[11]

Another sign of trust is delegating significant decisions. Although it is important to delegate decisions that are manageably difficult for individuals, it is usually a mistake to begin by delegating the safest, relatively trivial ones. Remember the importance of meaningfulness in self-management? Your team members are likely to see the delegation of trivial decisions as a sign of low trust, and to learn that self-management is not very meaningful.

Finally, it is a good idea to express your trust out loud by actively encouraging team members to take on new responsibilities. This is especially important for workers who have been micromanaged for long periods and are concerned about taking this new risk. When you delegate significant authority, then, it is useful to tell team members why you have the confidence to give them that authority. David McNally has discussed this sort of encouragement by using the metaphor of young birds testing their wings and learning to fly. His message is reflected in the title of his book, *Even Eagles Need a Push*.[12]

Providing Security (and Allowing Honest Mistakes)

Drive out fear.
—W. Edwards Deming[13]

You do not lead by hitting people over the head—that's assault, not leadership.
—Dwight D. Eisenhower[14]

A sense of choice requires that workers feel safe to make what appear to be the right decisions—to experiment, adapt, and innovate. Recall that this sort of problem solving is one of the main advantages of self-management. Allowing innovation, in turn, means that some mistakes will happen. As leader, you can do what you can to reduce unnecessary mistakes by matching how much you delegate to your judgment of team members' abilities. You can also keep informed and be available to help them (without retaking control) if they need your help. But you cannot avoid all mistakes if you want the benefits of self-management and intrinsic motivation. When workers try out new solutions, for example, their experimentation necessarily involves some trial-*and-error* learning.

Progress and learning, then, mean expecting and allowing some honest mistakes—and using them as important learning opportunities. If workers are afraid of being punished for honest mistakes, in contrast, they are likely to play it safe and stay very close to well-established, tried-and-true solutions. Team members will be afraid to trust their judgment, and work will become less about doing the task in the best possible way and more about not getting in trouble. When that happens, you are back to a conservative conformity, despite your delegation of authority.

Here again, there is a trap that some leaders and entire organizations fall into. In the military, it's called a *zero-defects mentality*. To be sure, there are a few tasks—nuclear power safety, for example—where mistakes can be catastrophic. On those tasks it is important to be vigilant for possible errors and to take a hard line with workers who allow them to occur. The trap is in extending this vigilance and punishment to tasks where mistakes are not catastrophic. When that happens, prevention of mistakes gets treated as a more important measure of effectiveness than making progress on the task purpose. What follows is an intolerance of mistakes that cascades down the organization. Leaders whose own jobs are on the line threaten their team members with punishment for mistakes. In their vigilance for mistakes, leaders are more likely to be seen as "playing gotcha" than supporting the team. Besides conformity, the common symptoms of the zero-defects trap are withholding information on mistakes, falsifying records, and a preoccupation with assigning blame.

The remedy, of course, is to actively support team members' rights to make intelligent mistakes. Honest mistakes, mistakes that make sense given the information at hand, need to be treated as *good* mistakes and used to produce learning. In *Thriving On Chaos,* management consultant Tom Peters described a number of well-run organizations where the value of speed and innovation is so well recognized that the organizations actually have awards for intelligent mistakes.[15] In organizations that do not have this philosophy, defending good mistakes by team members may take more courage on your part. You may have to take the heat for those mistakes, defending them on the basis that they were risks worth taking and that they resulted in significant learning.

Providing a Clear Purpose

Alice went on. . . . "Would you tell me, please, which way I ought to go from here?"
"That depends a good deal on where you want to get to," said the Cat.
—Lewis G. Carroll[16]

The first three building blocks—delegation, trust, and security—give workers the freedom to make choices. But freedom alone won't allow workers to make effective and rewarding choices. The two remaining building blocks—clarity of purpose and information—allow workers to make informed choices. Without these factors, choice can become anxious guesswork, providing more stress than satisfaction.

I have already discussed the importance of purposes to a sense of meaningfulness. The point here is that a clear purpose is also needed to enable choice—as the quote from *Alice in Wonderland* suggests. That is, team members need to understand what defines success on a task before they can decide what path to take to get there. As leader, then, you need to make sure that you and your team members share the same understanding of long-term purposes and more intermediate task goals, without your getting too far into the weeds about how to meet those goals.

Providing Information

Management must think we're mushrooms—they keep us in the dark and feed us bullshit.
—Anonymous

People without information cannot act responsibly.
—Ken Blanchard, John Carlos, and Alan Randolph[17]

If team members are to make good choices—and get satisfaction from making those choices—they need access to all sorts of relevant information: technical information, customer information, upcoming changes, and so on. So as you delegate more and more decisions, you will find yourself thinking less about what *you* need to know about those matters, and thinking more about what your team members need to know. You will shift significantly from making decisions to the support role of making sure your team members are informed. At G.E., the principle is to push decisions down to the lowest level where ability and information exist, and then to ask pointedly, "If they don't have the information, why not?"[18]

As a leader, you generally have a wider range of contacts outside the unit and more access to strategic information from upper management than your team members have. You will need to relay useful bits of information from these contacts to your team, of course. (You'll also find yourself responding to information requests from your team.) But as you delegate more, you'll also want to make sure that your team members get wired into their own networks so they can get the information they need more directly and quickly—or else you'll become an information bottleneck. This means helping them get on-line access to relevant accounting, customer, or other databases, as well as getting introductions from you into the informal network of relationships that may be helpful for their decision making.

Building Choice in Your Own Job

Now, what can you do to create these same building blocks for choice in your own job?

Negotiating for the Authority You Need

> *Control your own destiny or someone else will.*
> —Jack Welch[19]

Once you commit to a purpose, it is extremely frustrating not to be able to use your intelligence to best achieve that purpose—to see better ways of achieving the purpose but be unable to do the right thing. In effect, you hold yourself accountable for achieving the purpose, but you can't control your own destiny and it eats your heart out.

The first step is to negotiate with your boss for the authority you need. In these negotiations, pay particular attention to the two concerns that your leader will most likely respond to: how the added authority would help you or your team achieve the purpose, and the ability you have shown to handle that authority. I'll discuss the first concern here, and the second later in this chapter, under "Earning Trust."

Do you need more authority? To make what specific choices? Here, I invite you to take a moment to identify any areas where a lack of delegation is getting in the way of your effectiveness.

- Does anything slow you down and keep you from making timely responses to events—waiting for decisions that you could make faster, waiting for unnecessary approvals of your proposed actions?
- Does anything limit your flexibility to meet customer needs or otherwise adapt to conditions you face—inflexible rules, one-size-fits-all procedures?
- Does anything prevent you from making the most effective use of your resources—not controlling your own budget, not being able to make hiring decisions?

If you answer any of these questions by describing a specific situation, then you have a case to make to your boss. Again, phrase it in terms of how it would make you or your team more effective in achieving the purpose you and your boss share.

Earning Trust

> *We live in a world where self-leadership—taking responsibility for knowing yourself and for engaging in deliberate thought and contribution—is increasingly becoming a virtue.*
> —CLIFF HAKIM[20]

Before your boss can delegate the authority you need, you need to earn your boss's trust. Basically, you build trust by showing that you can handle that authority—that you are able to self-manage responsibly. Here, the elements of self-management provide a more detailed way of discussing your ability to self-manage: your commitment to the task purpose, and your ability to make intelligent choices, to perform competently, and to make progress on the purpose. These elements also provide a way of assessing your continuing development, so you need to have candid discussions with your boss around these issues.

What if the boss agrees that you could handle the additional authority, but is unwilling to delegate it to you because then it would be necessary to give it to everyone, and "some of your peers couldn't handle it"? Then your boss is buying into a one-size-fits-all style of delegation. Point out the importance of delegating authority based on individual or team levels of development in self-management. Suggest this as a solution to the dilemma— as a way to give you the authority you need to perform better, provide an explanation for others, and focus attention on what others could do to earn more authority.

Not Yielding to Fear

The only thing we have to fear is fear itself.
—FRANKLIN D. ROOSEVELT[21]

Never act out of fear.
—ANONYMOUS

Fear can cause people to give away their choices and power, leaving them feeling dependent on other people and events outside their influence. To be sure, there are realistic fears that need to be acted upon. But the danger is in the *unrealistic* fears that keep us from thinking clearly and acting out of our own intelligence. Psychologists tell us that some of our strongest fears are left over from childhood—when we were small and dependent, and there were scary things around that we couldn't handle. Although we are adults now, some situations can still trigger those old fears, even though we are no longer small and helpless. If we act on those fears, we wind up avoiding choices (or making bad ones), and we strengthen the power of those fears over our lives. It is useful to treat fear as a warning signal, not as truth. Examine it and talk it through with trusted friends, rediscovering your power. Then act, but out of your best thinking, not out of the fear.

Are there any fears that keep you from using your intelligence to choose new or better ways of doing your job? Of doing the right thing to advance the task purpose? How real are those fears?

How about the fear of breaking rules? A few years ago, I had the pleasure of interviewing Admiral Bill Rowley, a visionary and empowering leader in naval medicine. He spoke at length on the need for people to take risks rather than mindlessly following rules if an organization was to excel in meeting its mission. "How about the fear of punishment?" I asked. His answer has stayed with me. He firmly believes there is no significant risk if you genuinely try to "do the right thing."[22] In cases when the rules prevent patients from getting the care they need, he pointed out, it is the bureaucrats who put patients at risk by blindly following rules who get into trouble. "Doing the right thing" stands up very well to scrutiny.

Take a moment to absorb this insight. Rules and procedures are imperfect guidelines designed to help the purpose get accomplished. When they get in the way and put the purpose at risk, you need to correct the situation by relaxing the rules or getting them changed. This is a situation where your organization *needs* you to act intelligently.

How about the fear of your boss's anger? Can you recommend changes in your boss's decisions when you are convinced they are wrong? Here's another military example. I recently spoke with a U.S. Marine officer who flies in large planes with sizeable flight crews. As you know, the marines have a strong respect for rank and authority. Nevertheless, it is vital that subordinates on the flight crew be able to assertively point out problems to the pilot during flight if they are to save lives. I learned that crew members receive training to be able to say things like the following: "It is my duty to you and our plane to tell you when something will hurt us," and then to give specific information.

Again, take a moment to try on similar words for dealing with your boss. You have a *duty* to your boss, as well as to the organization and your task purpose, to point out dangers. Notice that this approach appeals to the mutual concern you and your boss have for the task purpose. Notice also that this approach avoids the issue of whether the boss's decision was right or wrong. Win-lose arguments about whether past decisions were right or wrong are pointless and destructive, like arguments over blame. This marine's approach is giving his boss new information that he believes is important to the boss and is likely to lead to a new understanding and decision. It works when you sincerely have the task purpose at heart, and when you can also listen to your boss's information in return. (I'll get back to this collaborative approach in Chapter Ten.)

Finally, consider the worst case. You have been negotiating with your boss but cannot get the authority you need and have earned. You are also trying to do the right thing but getting punished for it. Then keep in mind that you do have other choices beyond this job—you can look for a transfer within the organization or for another organization where you could use your judgment in the service of a meaningful purpose. After all, this is a new labor market, where organizations compete on their ability to attract and keep self-managing people. If your experience is typical in this organization, you won't be the only good person to leave. Why would you want to stay?

Clarifying Your Purpose (and Seizing Opportunities)

People like you and me may become giants. Giants see opportunity where others see trouble.
—MAX DEPREE[23]

Making intelligent decisions, as noted earlier, requires a relatively clear purpose. Yet in the new work world, you are likely to encounter more and more ambiguity. Your delegated tasks are likely to be stated in more general ways, to give you the flexibility to handle unexpected events. And the pace of change is increasing, so you will be bumping into more unexpected situations that weren't planned for—that aren't clearly covered by your purpose. This ambiguity means that you will need to keep clarifying and reinventing your purpose as you meet these new circumstances. Looked at another way, change presents you with opportunities to advance your vision in new ways. If you can think of it this way, change becomes a sort of Easter egg hunt where you try to spot and seize these opportunities—rather than an avalanche that threatens to bury you in debris.

Take a moment to think about any changes you are facing at work. What opportunities are there that you could get excited about? What specific purposes could you take on to capitalize on these opportunities?

To be sure, you will need to coordinate with your boss as you spot these opportunities. But don't be shy here. The organization needs you to take initiative in this area. *You* are the person on the scene—the organization's advance party. You are the best person to seize on these opportunities and to find a way to harness them to your unit's purpose.

Getting the Information You Need

Information about business strategy, processes, events, and business results . . .
—Edward Lawler[24]

Let me describe an old compliance-era dilemma. Many command-and-control bosses didn't want their people "bothering" people outside their function and required all questions to go through them. So subordinates asked their bosses a few, select questions, but limited them so they wouldn't seem pesky or stupid. Feeling that they were somehow supposed to know these things, they were forced to make many guesses and then to wait rather anxiously to hear how well they had guessed.

Luckily, the new information rules are quite different in most organizations. Hierarchies are flatter, and contacts across departments are encouraged. The norms now call for people to talk to whoever has the information they need to make sound decisions. That means direct contact with people in other functions and often with people at different organizational levels in those functions. Increasingly, it means going outside the organization to get information from customers and suppliers. It also means having access to computerized networks and databases that link people throughout an organization, and often between organizations.

So take a moment to ask yourself if there are still some areas where you are guessing because you don't have access to information you need. If so, what would you need? An improved information system? A better database? Introductions to a few people? How can you help make this happen?

9

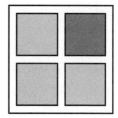

Building a Sense of Competence

You have a sense of competence on a task when you feel that you are performing your work activities well—when your performance of those activities is meeting or exceeding your own standards. At such times, you are also likely to feel pride in the good work you are doing. If you are working on a product, feelings of competence may show up as a sense of craftsmanship, workmanship, or artistry. If you are performing a service, the feeling of competence may show up as a sense of responsiveness in handling the events and conditions you encounter. When you feel a sense of competence, you are also likely to feel a mastery of the task activities you are performing and a confidence about being able to handle them in the future. You are also likely to find yourself deeply engaged in performing the activity—paying close attention to your task activities as you deal with the requirements and challenges of the moment.

When you feel little sense of competence, in contrast, you tend to feel little pride in your performance of work activities. A low sense of competence can come in a number of forms. You may simply not care about these work activities and not be trying especially hard to do them well, so that you take little pride in them. You may care about these activities but not be able to meet your standards for any number of reasons that have little to do with your ability, leaving you feeling embarrassed or dissatisfied by the quality of your work. You may find yourself dealing with challenges that are beyond the skills you have developed so far, feeling overwhelmed or anxious. At the other extreme, you may have mastered your task activities so well that you are no longer challenged by them, so that you are doing things on automatic pilot and no longer getting much satisfaction from a task that seems so easy that it's trivial.

Understanding the Sense of Competence

Performing task activities is the most visible part of most jobs, so many writers have offered explanations of what makes this performance rewarding. A number of related terms have been used, including competence, mastery, artistry, and engagement. I'm using the more established term *competence,* but this intrinsic reward is complex and often includes bits of the other related feelings as well.

The idea that performing activities well is intrinsically rewarding became popular in the late 1950s, when psychologist Robert W. White wrote a classic article, "Motivation Reconsidered: The Concept of Competence."[1] Even infants, he noted, take pleasure in learning to master skills and keep doing things for the *simple pleasure of doing them well.* This sense of competence motivation, he argued, is built into all of us to help us acquire the skills that we need to survive and to thrive as a species. In the 1970s, Edward Deci began publishing psychological research that showed how a sense of competence can keep people engaged in anagrams (word scrambles) and other activities.[2] (Deci's model is briefly described in Appendix A.) Getting positive feedback about doing something well is often enough to keep people performing an activity—doing it for the sheer pleasure of enjoying the resulting feelings of competence. The power of this reward is apparent in the universal popularity of recreational games. There are even a number of pastimes—like spectator sports and some performing arts—where much of our reward comes from the pleasure we get in seeing other people show great competence.

In the context of a meaningful purpose, performing activities well takes on an added significance. If you are pursuing a meaningful purpose, and you have chosen activities that you believe will accomplish that purpose, then performing those activities well also means that you are *serving that purpose.* In other words, you are aware that performing well is making an important difference in achieving something you care about. Consider surgeons at work in an operating room. They may be enjoying their skill and dexterity, but a large part of that enjoyment is in knowing that the competence of their actions is helping a patient.

I find that some of the sense of competence also involves a kind of aesthetic or artistic satisfaction, as though we were all artists creating things in different media. That is certainly true for me as I am writing this section of the book. I am trying my best to express these ideas clearly—to clarify the ideas and to pick the right words—and to make the sentences flow. When it seems to be going well, I get a sense of artistry that helps to sustain me. My inner voice says things like "Yes, that's a nice sentence" with an intensity that ranges from satisfaction to excitement. Consultant Dick Richards has described this experience of artistry in his wonderful little book, *Artful Work.*[3] Like artists, we gradually master the fundamentals of our various crafts—that is, we learn to be technically sound—and then learn to improvise and create new variations to meet the uncertainties that the new work brings us. We are used to the idea of craft workers' being artisans, so that the word *craftsmanship* suggests a kind of artistry. However, service work can also involve artistry. For example, there is a competent way of handling difficult customers well that I can only describe as "graceful." The same is true for skilled teachers. The relationship between competence and artistry also holds for managerial jobs, as spelled out in Peter Vaill's book, *Managing as a Performing Art.*[4]

Research also shows that we tend be most engaged in the task when we are performing activities most competently—having all our attention on meeting the challenge of the activities we are performing. This state of psychological involvement or engagement helps us perform well, but is also a positive experience in itself. It is characteristic of peak performance.[5] When people become fully engaged in doing good work, they become so engrossed in the task that they often lose track of time and are surprised to learn how quickly it has flown by.

Finally, we may also have feelings of virtue when we are meeting our own standards of competent performance. We stand a little taller as we feel that we are "doing it right."

Leading for Competence

Now, how can you help build a sense of competence for your team members? There are five building blocks for competence:

- Knowledge
- Positive feedback
- Skill recognition
- Challenge
- High, noncomparative standards

Providing Knowledge

Management Principle #6: Institute training on the job.
—W. EDWARDS DEMING[6]

Over time, workers gain a great deal of knowledge through their own experience with a task—through experimentation and feedback. Some of this knowledge is implicit or *tacit*—difficult to express, like how to perform a physical skill gracefully. The rest is *explicit* knowledge that can be expressed and shared. This explicit knowledge includes learnings about techniques, best practices, and rules of thumb that contribute to competent performance. Adding to this knowledge can be a relatively quick way of increasing competence—allowing workers to jump ahead of where they would otherwise be on their own learning curve.

As a leader, you'll probably need to provide some of this knowledge through relevant training courses. See what's available. But you'll probably also want to harvest and transfer some of the knowledge that already exists in your team or elsewhere in the organization. A variety of techniques are now available for surfacing and sharing knowledge in this age of "learning organizations." However, the basic idea is to help team members get in contact with others who have developed some competence in the same or related tasks. What can they learn from each other and from you? Who else outside your team, or even outside your organization, is a resource?

Providing Appreciative Feedback

The worst mistake a boss can make is not to say well done.
—JOHN ASHCROFT[7]

Workers must be able to monitor the competence of their ongoing activities in order to make adjustments in their performance. Much of this feedback is available to workers as they interact with a product or customer, but some needs to be measured more elaborately. Under self-management, workers need to be given the tools and data needed to assess the quality of their performance and to make adjustments themselves whenever possible.

Even so, there are likely to be some aspects of performance that are hard to assess and adjust without help. This is the reason we need coaches to help us improve our tennis, for example. There are things I simply cannot see well about my tennis serve that a coach can see more easily. So, as leader, you will often be able to provide helpful coaching to team members. As you provide this coaching, keep in mind that the psychology of coaching is quite different from the micromanagement of the compliance era. If the other building blocks are in place, workers will care about the competence of their work, will feel in charge of their performance of activities, and will be responsible for their own competence. In that context, you are there as a resource to offer observations that may help them.

As you give feedback, it is important to be aware of the dangers of deficiency focusing—discussed in Chapter Seven. In a given situation, you can choose to focus on the positives or the negatives, for there will usually be both. Saying that someone is doing things 99 percent well is experienced differently from saying that 1 percent of their work is substandard, even though both statements may be true. It is clear from the research done by Edward Deci and his colleagues that positive feedback increases the sense of competence, while negative feedback undermines it.[8] In addition, it appears that people are much more sensitive to negative feedback than to positive feedback. So, if one of your purposes is to amplify the sense of competence of your team members, you will want to focus on the positive that is being accomplished through their efforts. This has been called an "appreciative" stance.[9] Again, you are not ignoring the room for continued improvement. You can help and encourage team members to keep improving their performance as you also recognize the competence and improvement that have been occurring. If you continually focus on the deficiencies that remain, in contrast, you will be consistently undermining your team members' sense of competence. Your comments will basically be experienced as punishing.

Recognizing Skill

This innate need for appreciation is not a selfish, superficial craving for the center spotlight; it is an authentic, deep-seated desire to be deemed as worthy when offering something of worth.
—TERRENCE DEAL and M. K. KEY[10]

When you give team members recognition for the competence of their work, you are doing a number of important things. For example, you are strengthening the message that good work is important, valued, and noticed. You are appreciating the effort and accomplishment involved—providing a kind of "thank you" for a team member's contribution on behalf of the team and the organization. But perhaps most important, you are also validating and amplifying that team member's sense of competence. For a moment, the two of you step back from the task activity, view the work in perspective, and together appreciate how well it was done.

It is important for you to be aware of any biases you may have that prevent you from appreciating the competence of your team members. Favoritism will breed cynicism and resentment, of course. However, there is another kind of bias that is also worth looking out for. Walt Tymon and I found in our research that some individuals are generally less likely to recognize competence than others. These people are quick to attribute good performance to other factors—an easy task, other people's help, or luck. Low scores on our measure of "skill recognition" were related to lower feelings of competence.[11] Look out for that tendency—it damages intrinsic motivation. You want to be generous in recognizing the competence of your team members.

Managing Challenge

What I have called flow experiences. . . . Athletes refer to it as being in the zone. . . . Flow tends to occur when a person's skills are fully involved in overcoming a challenge that is just about manageable.
—MIHALY CSIKSZENTMIHALYI[12]

People perform best when there is a fit between their ability and the task difficulty, or challenge. If the task is too easy, their attention wanders and they become bored. If it's too difficult, they get anxious and do less than their best work. An ideally challenging task is just manageable and requires full concentration. Because the task is challenging, it inspires even more satisfaction when it is performed well. Recently, the psychologist Mihaly Csikszentmihalyi, whose name is itself a challenge, has written a number of books on the fit between skill and challenge.[13] He reports that people are most likely to be fully engaged in their task activities when skills and challenges are both high and matched. He refers to this experience of full engagement as a sense of "flow"—what others have called being "in the zone."

As leader, then, you'll want to try to keep your team members close to this condition of optimal challenge. One way you can do this is through task assignments, making sure that skills are adequate to the difficulties of the task, but that the difficulties are challenging. Another way is by helping to set even higher, more challenging standards as the team gets more skilled at its tasks.

Fostering High, Noncomparative Standards

No one can enjoy his work if he will be ranked with others.
—W. EDWARDS DEMING[14]

In the self-management of the new work, standards of competence have to be internalized by workers. Standards have to matter to workers—to be important to them—if workers are to strive for standards and feel rewarded by meeting them. This caring about competence, of course, won't be independent of the other things they care about. So, as leader, it will be useful to think about helping to create a culture of competence in a team. This means making sure that team members see the connection between competence standards and the other things that the team cares about—specifically its vision, its values, and its understanding of customer needs.

As you talk with your team members about these standards, you'll probably find that some of the standards your team cares about will tap into core values that attracted people to this career and organization to begin with. Consider the differences between the Marine Corps, the nursing profession, engineering, and the arts. Each embodies different virtues or types of standards, and attracts people who value those virtues—courage and loyalty, compassion, precision, and creativity, respectively. What virtues or work values are most important to your team members? If you're not sure, you'd better talk with them about it.

Some performance standards may be obvious, and will serve to provide minimum competence standards. Encouraging higher standards is an important part of building a culture of competence, but it is often impossible to spell out those standards in detail because of the uncertainties involved in the new work. For this reason, many leaders use lots of stories about competent acts to give workers concrete examples. Such stories get retold to new workers and become part of the team's culture. For example, James Collins and Jerry Porras, in *Built to Last,* explain how Nordstrom gives its employees the single standard of "outstanding customer service" and tells them to use their good judgment to achieve it. But new "Nordies," they add, are also told story after story to help make this standard real—stories about cheerfully giftwrapping items purchased from other stores, for example, and about ironing a shirt for a customer who needs it that afternoon.[15]

As you work at fostering high standards, it is important that you embody those standards yourself. This leadership by example provides a visible model for team members—a role model for others to copy. Team members may begin adding stories about your performance to the team's culture. Embodying your team's standards also builds your credibility—your moral authority. If you hold yourself to a lower standard—for whatever reason—your statements on competence will seem hypocritical and are likely to be disregarded.

Finally, it is important not to let the personnel system drive your team members' sense of competence. W. Edwards Deming pointed out the dangers of performance systems that force ranked comparisons of workers, or enforce a grading curve—so that the competence of the average worker gets mathematically set at "mediocre." Your goal, after all, is not to have a team who see their work as mediocre or average. Rather, the ideal would be to have a team of high performers who feel proud of their work but who also understand that promotion slots and merit raises are limited. While I was on the faculty of the Graduate School of Business at the University of Pittsburgh, I was fortunate to have a dean, Gerald Zoffer, who was skilled at that balance of recognition and practical understanding. I received a number of appreciative letters and notes from him, which helped my sense of competence. Then when the time for merit pay increases arrived, we would all receive letters which began by apologizing for the limited pool of available funds, which he emphasized was less than we deserved given the high quality of work by our faculty. That approach worked well for my intrinsic motivation. By contrast, I know of other leaders who feel obliged to begin criticizing work competence early in the performance cycle so that workers will accept the modest pay raise as justified. What a motivational waste!

Building a Sense of Competence in Your Own Job

If you are a team leader, some of your sense of competence will come from how competently your team performs its activities. Here, I'll concentrate more on the sense of competence you get from performing your own activities well.

Getting the Knowledge You Need

> *All men who have turned out worth anything have had the chief hand in their own education.*
> —SIR WALTER SCOTT[16]

Much of your learning will come from your own experimentation and the feedback you receive. But it would be very inefficient to limit yourself to this type of direct learning. You'll want to find out what other experts have learned and see how it will help you. Remember the feedback arrows in the self-management model in Figure 5.1? Feedback can lead you to improve the way you perform activities or to choose new activities that will result in better performance. New knowledge can give you new ways of doing both—giving you options that would take you a long time to discover for yourself.

Although it may be difficult to find the time to seek out this knowledge, this is a high-leverage path for increasing your own sense of competence. Take the courses you need, read books and articles, and find your own experts. The quality movement has taught us the value of benchmarking high-performance organizations and learning their lessons. Do the

same for individuals whose competence you respect—either peers or superiors. If it's a peer, buy lunch for the two of you and try a knowledge exchange, which may develop into a friendship. If it's a superior, try out a
mentoring relationship. Either way, there will be rewards for the experts
you've chosen as well as for you. Your interest will serve as a form of recognition for them, and sharing their learnings will amplify their own sense
of competence. So—once again—don't be shy here.

Getting the Feedback You Need (and Listening)

The need to know and the fear of knowing. . . .
—ABRAHAM MASLOW[17]

There may be areas where you'll need to ask for feedback on your activities. If running meetings is an important part of your job, for example, you
may want to begin holding brief "postmortems" after each meeting to get
feedback on the meeting. You may also be able to bring in consultants or
other coaches to provide feedback on some of your activities.

However, it is likely that you already get a fair amount of feedback directly from many task activities. You get many clues to tell you if you are
explaining things well to a team member, for example, or if you are handling negotiations with a customer well. In most cases, you also receive suggestions from the people who depend on you. If most of the building
blocks are in place, for example, your team members will care about the
competence of their work and about their task purposes, so that they will
let you know what you can do differently to help.

In many ways, competence depends on listening to this feedback—
even though, as the quote that opens this section suggests, everyone feels
ambivalent about getting evaluative feedback. The importance of the feedback is obvious—it contains information you need to improve your competence. My friend and colleague Barry Leskin likes to say, "When you're
in trouble, the facts are friendly." A recent book by Janelle Barlow and
Claus Moller, *A Complaint Is a Gift,* conveys a similar message about listening to feedback from customers.[18] Accepting valid feedback is also part
of your integrity—and it encourages honesty in your team members. If
you suppress feedback or don't act on it, your team members will eventually stop telling you the truth.

Still, getting negative feedback can hurt. Try to focus on the fact that the feedback is about helping your performance. If, on the other hand, the feedback given within your team does seem to be especially negative and hurtful, it's probably time for some team training on constructive, appreciative feedback.

It will also pay to take responsibility for giving yourself appreciative feedback. When you can, take a moment after an activity—especially an important or especially difficult one—to give yourself some recognition. Again, look out for deficiency focusing. For those of you who *are* deficiency focusers, I'll share some personal history here. Years ago, before I started doing research on the topic, I realized that I had a built-in assumption that I "should" be problem solving whenever possible—scanning for difficulties or shortcomings and figuring out how to deal with them. This kind of thinking had become a strong habit—and one that often left me anxious and dissatisfied. It occurred to me rather suddenly at one point that my assumption was the problem! So I began very deliberately to spend more time noticing what was working well and celebrating it—even though it felt uncomfortable at first. That change in thought patterns has made a surprising difference in my intrinsic motivation and in the general quality of my life. If you are a deficiency focuser, increasing your sense of competence may be as simple as giving yourself permission to enjoy your good work, and then putting that decision into practice. Catch yourself doing well!

Recognizing Your Own Skill

You see, you can't please everyone,
So you've got to please yourself.
—RICK NELSON[19]

If you are fortunate, you'll receive recognition from team members, your boss, and others. When this happens, my advice is simple: *let it in!* Look out for the "Yeah, but—" reflex. "Yeah, that went well, but I almost dropped the ball." Or, "Yeah, I pulled that off, but let's see how I handle tomorrow's meeting." That reflex is a way of negating the recognition and your own sense of competence. If you find you do this, try practicing phrases like, "Thank you. That did go well, didn't it."

Still, it's impressive how often the word *thankless* is applied to many tasks. Clearly, you can't always depend on others' recognition. You'll need to recognize your own skill. Here again, look out for any tendency you may have to exaggerate the importance of things other than your skill—luck, others' help, or an easy task. Don't short yourself here. Recognizing your competence is important to your intrinsic motivation and also allows you to confidently take on the kinds of challenges you can handle.

Managing Challenge in Your Own Work

*One must learn to balance the opportunities for
action with the skills one possesses.*
—MIHALY CSIKSZENTMIHALYI[20]

The trick here is knowing how and when to say no—and when to take on more challenge. When your plate is full or you are unable to meet your own standards, you have to be able to resist additional assignments. (Chapter Ten will discuss collaborative approaches to these negotiations.) The alternative is to stretch yourself so thin that you violate your own standards in order to simply get it done—or else burn yourself out trying to do it all. When you face such a request, one approach is to lay out your current projects and your standards, so that the other person understands how the request would affect your performance.

On the other hand, if things are running smoothly, you are in danger of losing interest. Then it's probably time to take on something more challenging. This may mean some new initiative in the team or an additional special project you take on in your peer work team. It also means beginning to talk with your boss about advancement possibilities that will keep you challenged.

Setting High Standards for Yourself

The quality of a leader is reflected in the standards they set for themselves.
—RAY KROC[21]

*This above all: to thine own self be true,
And it must follow, as the night the day,
Thou canst not then be false to any man.*
—SHAKESPEARE[22]

The first quote that opens this section is from the man who built McDonald's, and states the importance of high standards for leaders. The second quote is from *Hamlet,* and tells us something about the foundation of all our standards for ourselves. In that play, old Polonius has been trying to impart some wisdom to his son Laertes, who is about to leave home. Polonius does this by trying to share some of the standards of conduct that he has learned. This last piece of advice is the central core of his wisdom—the importance of integrity and honesty. The quote illustrates several important truths.

First, it's hard to talk about standards, and especially leadership standards, without discussing issues of character. Good leadership—like good work of any kind—is not about cutting corners, doing what is expedient, or going for flash or form instead of substance. Good leadership and good work in general is what works over the long term, what meets the test, and what stands up to close examination. Your character is shaped by the degree to which you ask yourself these same demanding questions. Ultimately, your sense of competence comes from being deeply honest with yourself. This self-honesty is the core of most moral codes and systems of ethics. You are the judge for your own sense of competence—and one who is hard to fool very long! So good work usually involves some soul-searching about whether you are doing things right in your own eyes. It's about being able to look at yourself in the mirror and stand tall. This is the essence of "To thine own self be true."

Polonius is also saying that, if his son is honest with himself, he'll soon discover the importance of being honest with others. Again, interpersonal honesty and integrity is a foundation principle of interpersonal conduct in virtually all moral systems. It is especially important in the new leadership role, where effectiveness means having credibility with workers who are more free to say no. For this reason, there have been a number of recent books about leadership that focus on character, credibility, and integrity.

The quote suggests one final truth. Polonius comes across as a bit of a windbag in the play, and his son is less than enthusiastic about listening to his father's wisdom. People, it seems, need to internalize their own standards of conduct as they find them relevant to their own experiences. You simply can't transmit these kinds of standards in lists. People have to be looking for them to recognize their usefulness and to translate them into their own circumstances.

If you are a leader, what does all this mean about clarifying your own leadership standards? It means that you need to keep asking yourself the important questions until you have clear standards that fit you and your circumstances. You can read a number of good books to suggest these standards. But you have to find the standards that fit. So keep taking the time to ask yourself the hard questions and to update your answers. What standards do you really use now to judge your leadership? What really are the most important ways that you can add value through your leadership activities? What would it look like to be doing them well?

10

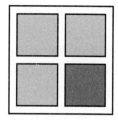

Building a Sense of Progress

You have a sense of progress on a task when you find yourself feeling encouraged about how well the task purpose is being achieved. You may experience this as a sense of well-being about having things on track and working out—a sense that you are in the midst of a successful endeavor. You are especially likely to feel in control of events at such times, as you see your task activities have the impact you intended. You also have the sense that all your time and effort on the task are paying off, so that you feel enthusiastic about the task and eager to keep investing your time and effort in it. If the task is especially meaningful for you, you are also likely to feel an excitement, or even a sense of wonder, about achieving an important purpose: "Yes! It's really happening!"

When you feel little progress, in contrast, you tend to feel discouraged about the task. You are likely to feel frustrated and stuck, sensing that the task purpose is slipping away. You feel less effective and perhaps even a bit helpless at such times, as events seem more outside your control. You find that it gets harder to keep up your enthusiasm and to keep exerting yourself on the task. If this continues, you are likely to burn out on the task eventually, and to see the task as hopeless. Far from being energized by the task, you begin to begrudge the effort you put into it—which now seems wasted or pointless—and to lose your commitment to the task purpose. If you remain on the task beyond this point, you are likely to become increasingly cynical and bitter.

Understanding Progress

Children tend to have an obvious and touching hunger for immediate gratification. On a car trip, they continually ask, "Are we there yet?" They want to be there now—wherever they are going. As people grow into adults, they generally learn to take on longer tasks and develop patience. But the need for reinforcement doesn't go away; it simply changes form. The childhood need to "be there now" evolves into the need to feel that you are getting there—that you are making progress. Monitoring the progress you are making on the task purpose is the final element of the self-management process discussed in Chapter Five. In many ways, progress is the bottom line of purposeful work. Is the purpose being realized or not, and how quickly? Having a meaningful purpose can be enough for you to begin a task with enthusiasm, but you need to keep experiencing a sense of progress toward that purpose in order to sustain that enthusiasm.

Some people ask me whether the ultimate intrinsic reward doesn't come from actually accomplishing the purpose—from the thrill of crossing the finish line. It is true that you may have the most intense positive feelings at that moment. For most meaningful purposes, however, climactic moments like this are a very small portion of your time on a task. Olympic athletes, for example, prepare four years for their brief moment of victory—and most of them lose the race or fail to make the team. It clearly takes some reinforcement along the way to keep them going. In addition, many task purposes don't seem to have clear-cut finish lines. For example, a committee may identify an important problem, collect information, draft a report, brief their recommendations to another group, see actions taken, and observe the gradual effects of those actions. Rather than having one big moment of triumph, there are a series of smaller steps forward—what Tom Peters calls "little wins."[1] On a day-to-day basis, then, it is this evidence of progress that keeps people going. So it seems more accurate to talk about a general need to make progress on a task, and to treat the final completion of the task as just one part of that progress.

Consider how central the notion of progress (or a lack of it) is to our experience of our tasks, and of our lives as a whole. As discussed in Chapter Four, people seem hardwired to think of themselves as on journeys. We ask each other, "How's it going?" We answer with phrases like "moving forward," "on track," "moving ahead," "getting there." If there is no progress, we say we are "stuck," "at a standstill," "in a rut," "going nowhere," or perhaps even "losing ground" or "backsliding." You can probably think of other words that capture this sense of progress.

The rate of progress on a task is also important. Jack Welch, CEO of General Electric, speaks vividly of the energy that he and his employees get from moving forward quickly on work tasks. "Speed," he says simply, "is exhilarating!"[2] Again, think of the words people use to describe their rate of progress on tasks. If progress is swift, we use terms like "stepping out," "cooking," or "smoking." If slow, we use other phrases: "plodding," or "barely making headway." Feel the difference in energy level between *plodding* and *cooking.*

Feelings of progress are problematic for many types of jobs. For example, I recall a workshop that Walt Tymon and I gave at a meeting of human resource professionals. When they completed our *Empowerment Inventory,*[3] they scored relatively low on a sense of progress. This was an important insight for them, and helped them to identify more clearly the vague sense they had that something was missing in their work. In the discussion that followed, they were able to pin down several building blocks for progress that were missing in their work—milestones, measurement of improvements, and celebrations—and to identify action steps they could take to provide them.

Feelings of progress are often problematic for managers as well. In the 1980s, for example, psychologist Harry Levinson wrote a classic article titled "When Executives Burn Out."[4] In it he referred to the "special kind of exhaustion" that managers are likely to feel when they expend energy with few visible results.

Leading for Progress

As a leader, you can contribute to your team members' experience of progress in a number of ways. You can help build a climate that supports progress, make sure that team members get a rich supply of evidence to measure progress, and take time to recognize and celebrate their progress. There are thus five building blocks of progress:

- Collaborative climate
- Milestones
- Celebrations
- Access to customers
- Measurement of improvement

Building a Collaborative Climate

Come let us reason together.
—ANONYMOUS

Over the years, I've done a lot of research on conflict. Perhaps you've already used the *Thomas-Kilmann Conflict Mode Instrument* that Ralph Kilmann and I developed. I'm mentioning that material again here because the amount of progress your team members make will depend heavily on how they deal with the inevitable conflicts that come up within the team. If they butt heads and compete with each other, for example, they will become obstacles to each other and slow each other down. As a leader, you will want to help build a collaborative climate in the team, where team members support each other's progress on important tasks.

Figure 10.1 shows a model of five "conflict-handling modes."[5] Conflict occurs when the concerns of two people appear to be incompatible—to interfere with each other in some way. When they attempt to deal with the conflict, then, their behavior can be described along two basic dimensions. They are assertive to the extent that they try to satisfy their own concerns. They are cooperative to the extent that they try to meet the other person's concerns. Note that these dimensions are independent: they are *not* opposites. As the figure shows, collaborating is both assertive and cooperative. It involves trying to find an "integrative" (or win–win) solution that completely satisfies both their own concern and the other person's concern—that allows them both to make progress on their tasks.

Some people are skeptical about the possibility of integrative solutions, so here is a familiar example from international relations. In September 1978, the Camp David accords settled a competitive dispute between Israel and Egypt over the West Bank region that Israel had taken in an earlier war. The breakthrough occurred at Camp David when President Jimmy Carter

FIGURE 10.1 Five Conflict-Handling Modes

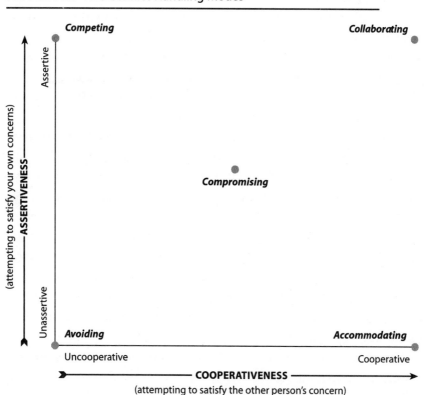

Source: Modified and reproduced by special permission of the Publisher, Consulting Psychologists Press, Inc., Palo Alto, CA 94303 from Thomas-Kilmann Conflict Mode Instrument by Kenneth W. Thomas and Ralph H. Kilmann. Copyright 1974 by Xicom, Incorporated. All rights reserved. Duplication in whole or part prohibited. Xicom, Incorporated is a subsidiary of Consulting Psychologists Press, Inc.

helped steer negotiations in a more collaborative direction. He helped each side identify its primary underlying concern—the thing it cared most strongly about. For Egypt, it was regaining sovereignty over its historic land; for Israel, it was the security of having a safe geographic area along its border. Realizing this, and gradually accepting the legitimacy of each other's concerns, they tried with President Carter's help to find a way of satisfying both concerns. The result was the return of the land to Egypt and the creation of a neutral United Nations force to maintain safety in that territory—an integrative outcome that advanced both sets of purposes.[6]

Consider what a collaborative climate means in a work setting. People listen to other team members' concerns, take them seriously, and try to facilitate them—as well as their own. Energy is directed into problem solving to advance all the tasks. To be sure, team members aren't always able to find integrative solutions; sometimes they have to settle for compromises. But they tend to make more overall progress than groups that never try. As a leader, isn't that the way you want your team to operate?

For contrast, consider the other conflict-handling modes and their effects on progress. *Avoiding* (unassertive and uncooperative) is a lose-lose mode: you don't address the conflict, so that you wind up neglecting both your own and the other person's concerns. When avoiding is prominent, tasks commonly get put on hold and little progress occurs. Competing, compromising, and accommodating are win-lose modes: you assume that both people can't win, so you focus on deciding who wins and who loses. *Competing* (assertive, uncooperative) happens when you try to satisfy your own concerns at the other person's expense. When competing is typical, energy gets directed against other team members, and there are many deadlocks that block progress. *Accommodating* (unassertive and cooperative) happens when you sacrifice your own concerns to satisfy the other person. When accommodating is the norm, people act cooperatively during meetings, but are usually left frustrated, which often leads to hallway complaining after the meeting and a lack of cooperation in actually implementing decisions. Finally, *compromising* (intermediate in assertiveness and cooperativeness) occurs when you settle for half a loaf—half of what each of you really wants. This mode results in expedient, partial sacrifices of both task concerns, leaving everyone with some progress, but less than they want.

For resources on building collaboration, see the notes for this chapter.[7]

Tracking Milestones

All motion is relative.
—Principle of physics

Consider what this principle means. You and I are whizzing through space at an incredible speed as we circle the sun, as the sun moves in its spiral galaxy, and as the universe keeps expanding. Yet this movement doesn't register for us because we don't have any fixed, visible reference points that we are passing. We need reference points to measure movement and progress. Chapter Seven discussed the importance of providing a detailed picture of a task vision so as to make work meaningful. The point then was that these details make the vision more real or compelling. Here, the point is that these same details provide the milestones that help you recognize that the purpose is actually being accomplished.

Milestones are especially important on longer tasks. Consider for a moment the difference between the task activities you perform and the task purpose you're pursuing. On a day-to-day basis, you do work activities and you watch for progress toward the purpose. On longer tasks, that progress is very gradual. There may literally be thousands of steps you need to take before you finish your part of the task. You know intellectually that each step advances the task, but there are so many steps to take that each step seems to make an imperceptible difference. It's a lot like taking a long hike. At the worst moments, the task can seem to go on forever, and you seem to be trudging. What you need, then, are milestones that mark recognizable progress and help keep you energized.

Milestones break up a task into psychologically significant advances. Think for a moment about why books like this one are divided into chapters. Clearly, one reason is to help you experience a sense of progress as you read through it—to reinforce your continued reading. I can also tell you that it is helping me, as the writer, feel a sense of progress as I write. As a leader, then, it is important to make sure that your team members have clear milestones—without lengthy gaps between them—to mark their progress on longer tasks.

As you help your team track milestones, keep in mind that some milestones toward the task purpose occur after your team's portion of the task is completed. For example, I find that I am still energized by news of the ongoing citations of some articles and the sales of a training instrument that I wrote over twenty years ago! Likewise, new proposals made by your team may be adopted and implemented by top management, or new products they have designed may be produced and sold. These downstream milestones are often the most important parts of achieving the task purpose. So it will be useful to continue tracking this progress and reporting it to the team.

Celebrating Progress

Without rite and ceremony . . . . Life becomes an endless set of Wednesdays.
—Lee Bolman and Terrence Deal, citing D. Campbell[8]

Some people are uneasy thinking about celebrations of progress. This seems to be one of those areas where our metaphors sometimes get in the way. People often talk about tasks as though they were short races—sprints. In a sprint, it is truly risky to celebrate your progress during the event. In the famous words of Satchel Paige, "Don't look back. Something may be gaining on you."[9]

The trouble is that most significant tasks in the new work world are not sprints. They may include a few stages that are like sprints, where there is intense time pressure to meet a requirement. But, overall, they stretch over a longer time frame and give team members time to plan and make choices—not just to perform task activities as swiftly as possible. On these kinds of tasks, then, people need to track their progress so as to make intelligent choices. Equally important, they need to celebrate their progress in some way to keep themselves energized.

A celebration is a time to pause, recognize that a significant milestone has been reached, and savor that fact. Recall that intrinsic motivation is about the energy produced by positive emotions about a task. Celebrations can be private, of course, but sharing them seems to amplify or intensify those emotions.

As leader, then, you can create a climate that encourages task celebrations, as well as starting some of those celebrations yourself. Sometimes it will be enough to simply pause during a meeting and note that an event is another sign of progress for the team. You may also want to briefly review the entire task to date, to show how far the team has come. I find that these simple "appreciative pauses" with colleagues have become very important during my own projects. Of course, some celebrations deserve to be more elaborate, depending on the significance of the event, the work schedule, and your organization's culture. Terrence Deal and M. K. Key provide some creative examples of celebrations in *Corporate Celebration*.[10]

Providing Access to Customers

The entire organization has to be structured so that employees can get feedback from customers about their performance and their responses to customer needs.
—Edward Lawler[11]

At a dinner show several years ago, I found myself seated next to a respected consultant who specialized in job design. When I mentioned that I was studying intrinsic motivation, he said something with such conviction that it has stayed with me: "The most important thing is to let workers work with customers." Ed Lawler, likewise, writes about giving workers a direct "line of sight" to the customer.[12]

The quality movement has emphatically reminded us that meeting the needs of customers, whether internal or external, is the main justification for work tasks. Earlier in the book, I discussed how the notion of helping customers is often what makes a task purpose meaningful. For that reason, customer satisfaction and appreciation is often the most direct evidence of ongoing task accomplishment.

There are a number of ways of getting evidence of customer satisfaction, of course. Sales figures, customer surveys, and letters of appreciation are important indicators of customer satisfaction. But for emotional impact, they are a poor substitute for direct, face-to-face encounters. There you can see the smile, feel the handshake, and hear the depth of feeling behind what the customer says. That's one of the reasons why politicians like to meet with constituents and "press the flesh." They aren't just winning votes; they're also reenergizing themselves. Likewise, actors and entertainers commonly speak of the energy they get from a live audience, as opposed to simply taping or filming a performance for the camera.

As a leader, then, you'll want to do what you can to provide workers with direct access to customers. Many jobs already have customer contact built in, of course. Researchers like Hackman and Oldham have shown that it is possible to build customer contact into a variety of other jobs.[13] For example, clerical workers who process insurance files can be given responsibility for contacting customers directly to resolve problems. At minimum, you can find ways of creating occasional meetings between your team members and some of the customers affected by their work.

Measuring Improvements (and Reducing Cycle Time)

Post measurements of progress conspicuously.
Simple, visible measures of what's important. . . .
—Tom Peters[14]

Recurring tasks are made up of cycles of activities. Another lesson from the quality movement is that measuring the outcomes of these cycles (how well the purpose is being achieved) gives workers the feedback needed to improve that cycle. In terms of the self-management model in Chapter Five, measuring whether outcomes are improving allows you to test the effectiveness of your choices, and to track the effects of work competence. Measuring the rate of improvement is also important to workers' feelings of progress.

The challenge here is to measure the right things. From a motivational point of view, you need to measure the outcomes that you and your team care about—those aspects of the task purpose that flow from your team's vision. These measures show the value added of your efforts in achieving that vision. Don't just settle for what's easy to measure. If you run training programs, for example, it is unlikely that your team members will get excited about simply offering more programs per year. What are you trying to accomplish with this training? How could you measure that convincingly? And, as the quote from Tom Peters suggests, why not post the results prominently?

In any measurement program, *cycle time* is one of the most useful things to track—and work to reduce. Ultimately, reducing cycle time is not about people running harder to cover the distance faster. It has more to do with redesigning and simplifying processes so that your team members have to cover fewer steps and climb over fewer obstacles. As noted earlier, eliminating steps that add little value to the task purpose makes work more meaningful, and eliminating unnecessary approvals increases workers' sense of choice. The point here is that these same improvements increase team members' sense of *speed*—helping them move from "trudging" to "cooking."

As leader, then, you will want to measure cycle time for key tasks and then to keep looking for ways of simplifying the processes involved—while enlisting team members' help. There are a number of tools for simplifying work processes, from suggestion boxes to process charting and reengineering.

Building Your Own Sense of Progress

Now, what can you do to craft these building blocks for your own sense of progress?

Building Collaborative Relationships

Think win/win; seek first to understand, then to be understood; synergize.
—Stephen Covey[15]

I invite you to think for a minute about any *non*-collaborative work relationships you may have that are interfering with your own task progress.
As you do this, try to avoid issues of blame, and to see these relationships
as opportunities to hone your collaborative skills. I'll offer a few how-to
suggestions here that have proven helpful for me.

First, I suggest that you announce your wish to make the relationship
more collaborative and, without blame, invite the other person to join you
in trying to make it happen. This sort of invitation can mark an important
transition point in a relationship. Without this step, any change in behavior from you may mystify the other person or even look like a trick. What
you're really doing here is trying to create new expectations about how to
handle the work issues that come up in your relationship. Be prepared to
explain how collaboration might help both your task purposes.

Then you'll need to begin with the nuts and bolts of the collaborative
process. Ask if this is a good time—and agree on another specific time to
meet if you can't go ahead right now. At that meeting, you'll need to confront the conflict issue—to start talking about it. (If you don't do this, you're
avoiding.) The important thing here is to begin this discussion by trying
to understand both sets of underlying concerns involved in the conflict.
Use active listening to understand the other person's concerns. Mirror back
what you are hearing until the other person agrees that you understand.
Then try to state your own underlying concern until the other person understands it. You will find that it will be easier to listen to the other person's concerns when you know that yours will be listened to as well.
Likewise, many people find it easier to state their own concerns when they
know that it won't be at the other's expense.

Once you both understand each other's underlying concerns, you'll
need to pose the conflict as a mutual problem: "Is there some way that we
can satisfy your concern for [x] and my concern for [y]?" As you offer your
ideas and invite the other person's ideas, it will pay to keep an open mind
and to be flexible about new solutions. Don't make the mistake of getting
locked into a competitive argument over solutions: "We should do [X]."

"No, we should do [Y]." The trick is to keep focused on your underlying concerns and to welcome any course of action that would satisfy them. In the negotiating literature, Dean Pruitt describes this stance as "firm flexibility"—being firm about satisfying your concerns, but flexible about solutions.[16]

As your behaviors in a relationship become more collaborative, you'll find that the relationship changes in other ways as well. Since collaboration is high in both assertiveness and cooperativeness, you'll find that you build both respect and liking for each other, and create a foundation for trust. This will make it progressively easier to handle future issues in a collaborative way—to help you both make progress together.

Developing Your Own Milestones

Mark milestones publicly: Post timelines and encourage people to color in their progress.
—TERRENCE DEAL and M. K. KEY[17]

Do any of your own projects seem to be dragging for lack of milestones? Stop a minute to think about where your team has come from and where it is headed. Do you have a clear idea of the stages involved in your vision for the team, and how to recognize them when they occur? Are you tracking those signs so you can recognize progress? Or consider a more specific project you are involved with. When was the last time you experienced a real sense of progress on that project?

It is easy to feel progress at dramatic transition points on a task—when groundbreaking occurs for a construction project, when a first draft of a report is completed, and so on. The rest of the time, you may need a more detailed route map of the project stages and substages to recognize that progress is occurring. On long stretches of repetitive work, you may need to create your own milestones to mark progress. When I do a swim workout, for example, I count laps and pay special attention when I reach a quarter of my target distance, the halfway mark, and the three-quarters mark. Those are psychologically significant points, and help keep my energy level up. Why not figure out when your project is approximately a quarter completed, half completed, and three-quarters completed?

Taking Time to Celebrate

Celebrate . . . the small wins.
—Tom Peters[18]

There are lots of ways of celebrating, and I'm going to assume that you can think of several. So rather than write about how to celebrate, I'm going to try to counter some of the concerns that keep people from celebrating. See if any of these statements sound familiar.

Concern #1: "It's childish." As I write this, I'm in my fifties, and have come to terms with the fact that part of me *is* still a child. The trick is to restate *childish* as *childlike*. Psychologists tell us that we carry our earlier developmental stages with us as we mature. The childlike part of us is the part that gets enthusiastic and excited about things—an important core of our energy. So from a motivational point of view, the last thing you want to do is to suppress that childlike source of energy. A better goal is to integrate it with your adult reasoning—to find ways of building that enthusiasm and harnessing it to the tasks that you care about. So why not give yourself permission to celebrate a little—to keep your energy and passion alive?

Concern #2: "If I slow down, I may stop." This is the "don't look back" idea I mentioned earlier. There's a kind of all-or-none reasoning connected with this concern: either I run full-out or I stop, so I'd better keep running hard. But even runners need to pace themselves. If they don't, they tie up and burn out. You're in this for the long haul, so pace yourself and take an occasional breather. Think of celebrations as investments and renewals, and as insurance against burnout.

Concern #3: "I don't want to brag." Some people are concerned about appearing prideful or provoking jealousy or resentment. But bragging is about how cool *you* are, while celebrating is about moving forward on a task. There's an important difference. If this is a concern for you, look for ways of celebrating modestly. Keep the task in the foreground. You can celebrate your "good fortune" if you like, which acknowledges that there was some luck involved. You can also reduce jealousy by sharing your celebration with teammates who shared in the task and with friends and family who genuinely care about you.

Making Contact with Customers

Non-sales employees are energized by the opportunity to serve customers directly.
—Bob Nelson[19]

I got to talk with the people who run the companies and tell them if they had complaints they should let us know.
—Steelworker cited by Bob Nelson[20]

These quotations are from Bob Nelson's book, *One Thousand and One Ways to Energize Employees.* The first is based on the experience of a shoe company that trains all its employees to be able to fill in for the sales staff in taking orders from customers. The second is a quotation from a melt-shop operator in a steel products company who was given the opportunity to travel with two salespeople. In both cases, meeting the customers gave people a chance to see what difference they were making for their downstream customers.

Stop for a moment to consider which of your customers are most important to you and your personal vision. Who would most lift your spirits by contacting you to let you know that you are making a real difference for them? This is often a complex question. Sometimes it's a group of end users far removed from you, sometimes an internal customer, a direct external customer, or your boss. And many leaders think of their team members as their most important customers.

Now, are there any of those important customer groups that you don't personally interact with? Or, if you interact with them, are there some with whom you don't discuss the differences you make for them? If so, how could you meet with these people and get the evidence you need to find out that your work makes a difference?

Measuring Improvements (and Tracking Intrinsic Motivation)

Anything worth doing is worth measuring.
—Principle used by Whole Foods[21]

Measuring improvements is important for a sense of progress at any long-term task. However, it is often difficult for leaders. Leadership is a relatively unstructured task in the sense that it isn't a simple, repetitive cycle of activities. So it is difficult to measure improvements in leadership very directly. I think of leadership as a matter of doing whatever is needed to help a team identify and achieve purposes, meet quality standards, and keep team members motivated. What this means is that measuring the value added of leadership boils down to measuring improvements in a team's achievement of task purposes, its work quality, and its motivation.

Notice that I've listed improvements in team members' motivation as one of three key measures of leadership. That is a logical conclusion from the premise of this book—the key role of intrinsic motivation in today's work. So if you are a leader and buy that premise, you'll want to keep tracking the intrinsic motivation of the people under your leadership. How else will you know whether they are energized by their work tasks, and what elements of intrinsic motivation still have room for improvement?

11

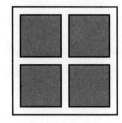

Implications

The past ten chapters have covered a lot of detailed information on intrinsic motivation at work. It's time for a recap and then a general discussion of implications.

A Brief Summary

A dramatic shift has been occurring in the nature of management and of work itself. People used to think of work in terms of the activities (behaviors) that workers needed to perform. Bureaucratic organizations used close supervision and elaborate rules to make sure that workers performed those activities properly, and the job of workers was mostly to comply with this sort of command-and-control management. By the 1980s and 1990s, however, the environment had begun to change too rapidly for bureaucratic rules and close supervision to handle. Those uncertainties overwhelmed bureaucratic organizations and forced a flattening of the hierarchy and drastic reductions in organizational rules. When this happened, work changed in fundamental ways. Workers have had to take responsibility for handling much of the uncertainty surrounding their jobs. Today's work is not simply about performing activities; it is now about workers' directing their own activities toward organizational purposes. The worker's role, then, has shifted from passive compliance to proactive self-management.

The motivational requirements of work have also changed. Self-management requires a deeper level of commitment than the old compliance-era work, since workers must now be committed to the purposes they are pursuing. The new work is also more psychologically demanding, involving a great deal more judgment and decision making. Although money and other extrinsic rewards remain important to workers, it is clear that the new work requires much more than that. Effective self-management depends heavily on intrinsic rewards—the psychological rewards that workers can get from self-management itself.

To understand intrinsic motivation, it's important to see the limitations of the rational-economic model that dominated motivational thinking in the compliance era. At its heart, intrinsic motivation is not about rational calculation—it is about passion and the positive feelings that people get from their work. These feelings reinforce or *energize* workers' self-management efforts and also provide the fulfillment that is needed to keep today's workers on the job. Building intrinsic motivation, then, is about finding ways to enable and amplify those feelings.

Recognizing the need for greater intrinsic motivation, organizations have been trying many different things, in a hit-or-miss way, to try to enhance that motivation. Likewise, career counseling books have promoted different strategies to help job holders find more rewarding work. What has been missing is a model of intrinsic motivation at work that spells out the key pieces of the intrinsic motivation puzzle and how they fit together. This book provides a model, together with diagnostics, to lead managers and workers from motivational problems to effective solutions.

Self-management depends on four key rewards: a sense of meaningfulness, a sense of choice, a sense of competence, and a sense of progress. The sense of meaningfulness and the sense of progress come from the task purpose—from the opportunity to pursue a worthwhile purpose and the perception that one is actually accomplishing that purpose. The sense of choice and the sense of competence come from the task activities—from the opportunity to choose activities that will best achieve the purpose, and from the perception that one is performing them well. These four rewarding feelings, then, can be thought of as "vital signs" for intrinsic motivation—as pulse rate and blood pressure are vital signs for physical health. A drop in any one of these four feelings is a sign of trouble. It is important that managers and workers be able to measure the levels of these feelings so that they can recognize motivational problems and find opportunities to enhance intrinsic motivation.

Effective diagnosis and action depend on knowing which reward is low, as well as the key building blocks for that reward—the conditions that allow that reward to operate at a high level. This book identifies five building blocks for each of the intrinsic rewards. When an intrinsic reward is low, then, any missing building blocks provide a way to pinpoint the source of that problem. Since these building blocks are shaped jointly by job holders and their leaders, this book has provided two sets of actions that can be taken to create each building block. One set of actions is for leaders to help craft the building blocks for their team members. The other is for job holders themselves, to help create the building blocks needed for their own intrinsic rewards.

Now, some general implications . . . from three points of view: for top managers, for leaders at all levels, and for individual job holders concerned with their own intrinsic motivation.

Implications for Top Managers

Intrinsic rewards are a key factor in keeping skilled workers, so the material in this book will be of special interest to top managers who are trying to reduce the loss of highly trained employees. Top managers of organizations with many professional service workers, or knowledge workers in general, are especially likely to see intrinsic rewards as a solution to their brain drain problems; however, the principles apply to other organizations as well. In addition, as Cliff Hakim has observed, retaining workers is a minimal goal.[1] The real power of intrinsic motivation is in having workers who not only stay, but stay because they are mobilized in the service of the organization's purposes—applying their passion, intelligence, and initiative. In this new world of uncertainty and international competition, an intrinsically motivated, self-managing workforce is a crucial resource for an organization— and one important source of competitive advantage.

Top managers necessarily have the lead role in building an organizational context for strong intrinsic motivation. Earlier in the book, I discussed the importance of commitment in any task. What would it mean for top managers to commit to achieving high levels of intrinsic motivation in their organizations? It would not mean saying and doing what one could and then hoping that intrinsic motivation would increase. It would mean systematically measuring intrinsic motivation and doing what was necessary to build and maintain it, just as those leaders do what is necessary to honor their other commitments. The four vital signs of intrinsic motivation—feelings of meaningfulness, choice, competence, and progress—would need to be tracked organization-wide to make sure that the efforts were actually working.

My colleague Erik Jansen likes to point out that top managers play a more central role in the intrinsic motivation of workers than they typically play in their extrinsic motivation. They can't simply ask the human resources department to put together an "intrinsic motivation package" for workers, or to design an "intrinsic compensation system." Intrinsic motivation depends heavily upon line managers' leadership from the top to the bottom of the organization, and the tone for this leadership must be set at the very top.

Because leadership is so important to intrinsic motivation, top managers need to make sure that team members' intrinsic motivation gets included as one measure of each of their leaders' performance. This means incorporating intrinsic motivation into the existing organizational systems that assess and *extrinsically* reward leaders at all levels. There's no contradiction here. Intrinsic and extrinsic motivation can support each other. If building intrinsic motivation is to be treated as one of a leader's purposes and responsibilities, then it would be foolish not to include it in the criteria for performance evaluation, promotion, and pay. (For a discussion of the role of pay, see Appendix B.)

However, it would be highly ironic—and ineffective—if top managers relied only on extrinsic rewards and punishments to try to force leaders in their organizations to lead for intrinsic motivation. Then leaders would likely comply only minimally with this program as another "check-the-box" requirement. And people would see that the top managers were not "walking their own talk."

With that in mind, let's consider some of the implications of the model of intrinsic motivation for making this happen. Leading for intrinsic motivation is a task for all the leaders in an organization—like any other task, with a purpose to be pursued and activities to be performed. The challenge for top managers is to provide a context that helps imbue this task with a sense of meaningfulness, choice, competence, and progress for those leaders. Here, then, are some guidelines that follow from the model:

Meaningfulness. It is up to top managers to state convincingly the strategic need for intrinsic motivation, to articulate the values and philosophy that support it, to incorporate it into their visions for their organizations, and to keep emphasizing that message. Let's be clear about this. Building intrinsic motivation is not just a nice thing for leaders to do for workers when they can. It is key to each worker's commitment, self-management, and innovation, and it contributes directly to the organization's achievement of its purposes. Top managers need to make sure people understand this.

Choice. It is important to allow managers to make their own choices about how to achieve this goal, so that they can use their ingenuity to make it happen and believe in what they are doing. It pays to encourage experiments. If top management provides a basic set of guidelines, managers should be allowed to adapt them to their own circumstances, so that they make sense for their situation.

Competence. It is vital to provide the necessary training, so that leaders throughout the organization understand the basics of intrinsic motivation. It will also pay to encourage the sharing of best practices across the organization and to recognize improvement and continued excellence in leading for intrinsic motivation.

Progress. Top managers should make sure that leaders at all levels get feedback on the intrinsic motivation of their teams. This can be done with surveys or incorporated into 360-degree appraisals.[2] Retention should also be considered here, since it is a rough index of intrinsic motivation.

I'd like to emphasize the importance of this last point—feedback on intrinsic motivation for leaders. I have seen the devastating longer-term effects of leaders who bullied their workers into short-term accomplishments, got promoted, and left the wreckage behind them. Somehow, the human costs of this leadership—plummeting intrinsic motivation, burnout, decisions to quit or transfer out—didn't get reflected in the evaluation of the leader. Often, seeing such leaders promoted by their organization was the last straw for team members who had suffered through the predator's stay, triggering a decision to leave the organization. Again, Jack Welch has talked about the need to confront such leaders with the consequences of their leadership styles:

> [That type of leader is] the most difficult for many of us to deal with. . . . Too often all of us have looked the other way—tolerated these . . . managers because they always deliver—at least in the short term. And perhaps this type was more acceptable in easier times, but in an environment where we must have every good idea from every man and woman in the organization, we cannot afford management styles that suppress and intimidate. . . . We know now that without leaders who walk the talk, all of our plans, promises, and dreams for the future are just that—talk.[3]

One more point—and this applies to leaders at all levels: *As you implement these ideas, please treat them as a set of guidelines and suggestions rather than a set of rules.* In other words, recognize your own choices and the role of your own ingenuity. If you commit to building intrinsic motivation, you will find yourself experimenting and making innovations. For example, a number of organizations—including Disney, Monsanto, and Shell—have developed "internal labor markets" that make it easy for employees to change teams when they see a new project that excites them.[4] See what innovations you can add.

Implications for Leaders at All Levels

Chapters Seven through Ten laid out specific action recommendations for leaders. Here, I'd like to emphasize a couple of more general implications of this model for leadership. The first point involves the importance of talking directly with team members about the rewarding feelings in this model.

Organizations have made major strides during the last two decades in recognizing the importance of feelings. Many, for example, make widespread use the *Myers-Briggs Type Indicator* for team-building sessions.[5] The *MBTI*, based on Carl Jung's theory of cognitive types, helps managers recognize the value of feeling as well as thinking in decision making.[6] I see the material in this book as another step in that same direction. I've tried to build a very logical framework for understanding the intrinsic rewards involved in self-management—to demystify them so that you can also use your intellect to deal with them. But at their core, these rewards are about strong feelings that keep people going—that keep them energized.

Being able to speak to these feelings is a key skill for today's leaders. A former colleague at UCLA, Mike McCaskey, summarized a number of research findings concisely: "groups run on emotion."[7] (He knows something about teams and motivation; he has since left academia to run his family business—the Chicago Bears football organization.) Talking with team members about those emotions allows leaders to help shape those emotions in ways that energize people. In Dick Richards's words, "the artistic medium of a leader is the energy of the followers."[8]

No inborn charisma is needed to do this. It's a matter of keeping the building blocks in mind while leaders talk honestly with their team members about four things they care about:

- The meaningfulness and significance of their task purposes
- Their choice of the best ways to accomplish those purposes
- Their competent performance of work activities
- The progress they are making toward their purposes

Those conversations allow leaders to take a rough, immediate measure of the levels of these "vital signs," as I have called them. They also allow them both to find out what building blocks may be missing—so that they can help provide them—and to help amplify these feelings where they can honestly do so. When Beverly Kaye, the retention expert and coauthor of *Love 'Em or Lose 'Em*,[9] read the first draft of this book, she wrote me the following words: "Imagine a staff meeting devoted to a discussion of what it takes to gain energy and commitment from each direct report. Meetings like this, and managers who commit to following on and following up, have a much greater chance to retain the talent on their team."[10]

The second point I want to emphasize is the flexibility of these ideas. They can be applied to any task within a work group. Leaders can apply these ideas to individual tasks or group tasks. In addition, "task" is a very elastic notion that can be used at different levels of generality. In dealing with an individual, for example, the ideas can be applied to an individual's entire job—to analyze and improve that person's overall level of intrinsic motivation and job satisfaction. It's at that level that one would be looking at how intrinsic rewards are affecting the person's intent to remain in the job and their overall performance. But these ideas can also be applied to a specific task the individual is working on—one project, for example. How committed and energized are they for that particular project, and why?

At the group level, leaders can use the model to analyze the overall motivation and performance of a team. How much self-management is going on in the group, and what is the general level of commitment? Or they can use the ideas to figure out why intrinsic motivation is low on a particular project group or for a particular ad hoc committee. Why did the New Products Committee lose its momentum after its first recommendation was rejected? The ideas can also be applied to a subtask—for example, to find out why people aren't filling out their expense reports on time. Are the reports seen as meaningless? Even a major change, say, implementation of a new computer system, can be viewed as a task, so that the model—with building blocks and leadership actions included—can be used to build intrinsic motivation and commitment for that change. In each of these applications, it's still a basic matter of understanding how meaningful individuals feel the purpose is, how much choice they think they have in figuring out how to achieve it, how competently they feel they are performing the task activities, and how much progress they feel they are making toward achieving their purpose.

Implications for Managing Your Own Intrinsic Motivation

Again, I've already covered a number of detailed action recommendations in Chapters Seven through Ten. So I'll focus on more general issues here.

I'll start by reminding you how important your own intrinsic motivation is. I'm talking about your energy level—the vitality you bring to work. That's crucial for your productivity and success at work. I'm also talking about how engaged and fulfilled you feel at work—the essence of your quality of work life and a large part of your overall quality of life. This is your work life—how much are you enjoying it?

I also want to reemphasize how incomplete and dangerous the old rational-economic model can be for your intrinsic motivation. Lots of us were raised to make the so-called rational decisions—to pick careers and jobs that would be relatively high-paying and dependable. We were also taught the importance of self-discipline and delayed gratification to keep us going when things got tough—and not to whine about it. Don't get me wrong. Making intelligent means/ends decisions is important, and self-discipline is important to get through temporary difficulties. But these decisions are not enough! And you shouldn't need self-discipline alone to keep you going from one end of your career to the other. It's also important to ask yourself regularly how much you're enjoying what you're doing and to take action to increase your enjoyment! What I'm talking about is also learning to take care of yourself in an important way.

My first recommendation, then, is to set high expectations for your own intrinsic motivation. The work world has changed, and the opportunities for intrinsically rewarding work are high—at all levels of the organization. Let this book show you what work can be.

Second, make sure that you check your job's four vital signs on a regular basis. At minimum, find some quiet time on weekends to reflect on your sense of meaningfulness, choice, competence, and progress. You may want to go over these vital signs with a trusted friend or mentor as well. When you find yourself feeling down about work, practice learning to identify which of these vital signs is lagging. And when you feel a surge of energy, learn to identify its source: "Wow, that's real progress!"

Third, take responsibility for your own intrinsic motivation. The old days of dependency and paternalism in organizations are all but gone, and people at all levels are more like partners. In Cliff Hakim's words, we tend to "join, not work for," our organizations these days.[11] Make sure you're not just waiting for someone else to fix things, or hoping that things will improve. This book has provided a set of building blocks and actions to help raise your intrinsic rewards. Figure out what's going on and make a plan to improve things. Your organization is also likely to benefit.

Finally, take action and track the results. Notice that raising your intrinsic rewards is a task. What I'm encouraging you to do, basically, is to learn to self-manage at this task—to commit to high levels of intrinsic reward for yourself, to use the material in this book to choose a plan of activities that will help raise those rewards, to keep taking action to implement those activities, and to keep monitoring your intrinsic vital signs to make sure that progress is occurring. Spend some of your energy on this task as an investment to increase your energy and your quality of work life and to set an example for the people around you.

Enjoy the adventure!

Appendix A

Two Earlier Models of Intrinsic Motivation

Why did my colleagues and I need to develop a new list of intrinsic rewards—didn't we already have models of intrinsic motivation? Yes, there were a couple of popular models dating from the 1960s. However, both these older models left out important intrinsic rewards that are central to the self-management process. I'll briefly describe them here so that you can see how the new model builds on them. (See the chapter notes for references to more detailed, academic discussions of the models.[1])

The most widely known model of intrinsic motivation was originally developed by Edward Deci, a psychologist at the University of Rochester.[2] Much of his later work on the model has been with Richard Ryan.[3] Deci recently wrote a popular book with Richard Flaste, *Why We Do What We Do,* which summarizes his views.[4] His model is based largely on a rigorous program of laboratory research involving experimental games such as anagrams (word scrambles). It is especially well known in the field of education. For my purposes, its main shortcoming is that the model focuses only on task activities as sources of intrinsic reward, so that purposes are excluded. In Deci's model, task activities are intrinsically rewarding when people experience a sense of self-determination (choice) and of competence. The model I've presented in this book builds on Deci's model by adding the rewards that come from task purposes, namely meaningfulness and progress. This is a key improvement in taking the model to work tasks involving more serious purposes. Deci has also made the controversial assertion that extrinsic rewards tend to reduce intrinsic rewards. Recent research reviews have found very little support for this effect, especially in organizational settings.[5] The current model sees no inherent conflict between intrinsic and extrinsic rewards. (For more on this idea, see Appendix B.)

The second model of intrinsic motivation was developed by Richard Hackman, now at Harvard University, and Greg Oldham of the University of Illinois.[6] It has been used widely in organizational settings, where it has largely replaced Frederick Herzberg's theory of motivators and hygiene factors.[7] The Hackman and Oldham model is often called the "job characteristics" model because it describes the effects of five dimensions of job design: skill variety, task identity, task significance, autonomy, and feedback. Research shows that these job dimensions generally have an impact on job satisfaction and other outcomes. However, there is less support for the motivational core of the model.[8] That part of the model says that intrinsic motivation occurs when three "psychological states" are present: experienced *meaningfulness* of the work, experienced *responsibility for outcomes* of the work, and *knowledge of actual results* of the work. For my purposes, there were two shortcomings to this list. First, it focuses only on task "outcomes" (similar to purposes) as a factor in intrinsic motivation, leaving out activity-related rewards. Second, only meaningfulness is clearly an intrinsic reward, as in the current model. Knowledge of results and responsibility for outcomes are only rewarding when those results are positive—that is, when progress is occurring. My current model, then, collapsed Hackman and Oldham's three psychological states into two intrinsically rewarding states—a sense of meaningfulness and of progress—and then added the missing activity-related rewards—a sense of choice and of competence.

Appendix B

Putting Money in Perspective

What is the role of money in an era of self-management and intrinsic motivation? People who study work motivation find it handy to separate two kinds of behaviors—*membership* behavior (joining an organization and remaining) and *performance* behavior (how one does the task). I'll start with membership behavior.

Taking a Job and Remaining

Consider the role of money in people's lives. For most of us, money isn't an end in itself, it's a means to satisfy other ends. There are some exceptions of course—people who measure their worth and success almost solely in terms of money. But for the vast majority of us, money is simply something that gives us choices for taking care of areas of our lives that are more important—including family and friends, our health, and rewarding work. We try to manage our finances with the goal of managing them well enough so that we have to make few important sacrifices to the things we value. Most of us don't try to maximize our money in isolation from our other needs, because we learn that this kind of single-mindedness can sacrifice our relationships with family and friends and our health, or lead us to take on work that is unfulfilling.

The importance of money in taking a job depends partly on the amount of financial cushion or slack you have—the difference between what you have and your basic needs. Again, that cushion gives you choices. With a large cushion, you can afford not to take the highest-paying jobs. You can take government service jobs or other lower-paying jobs with high intrinsic rewards, try self-employment, or even do primarily volunteer work. With no cushion, on the other hand, you may have to take the first job that comes along or to choose among jobs based on money alone. For most of us in between, with some cushion, money is a significant consideration in taking a job. We want pay and benefits to be in the range for comparable jobs—that is, to be fair. And more pay is better than less. But modest differences in pay are outweighed by differences in the intrinsic rewards that the jobs offer.

My experience, then, is that intrinsic rewards play a strong role in shaping most people's careers. People pick careers they believe will be intrinsically rewarding and choose to stay on a job or not based largely on the intrinsic rewards they actually receive. When those rewards decline, they get unhappy and start looking for other, more rewarding jobs. Large increases in pay (in new "career opportunities") can also direct them to new jobs within their career of choice, and unfair pay can cause them to begin looking for other jobs. But it is the intrinsic rewards that flow from the day-to-day work that tend to keep most of us coming back to a job.

Performing Well

What makes workers perform well? It depends on what you mean by "performing well." If you only mean following directions—that is, compliance—then extrinsic rewards will fill the bill. Make a sizeable part of pay dependent upon compliance, find a way of verifying compliance, and that should do it. But you'll have to live with the familiar pathologies of extrinsic reward systems—your workers will be doing things only well enough to get by, neglecting what is not measured, and finding ways of gaming the system.

On the other hand, if performing well means self-management, then you'll need intrinsic motivation. This sort of motivation involves commitment to the task itself. It comes from doing what one honestly believes is best for promoting the task purpose and work quality. It motivates workers to deal with uncertainties in the new work that can't be anticipated by the people who design pay systems. It also motivates workers to do their best even when nobody is looking.

As I was finishing this book, a study was published that is relevant here.[1] That study measured the combined effects of pay-for-performance systems and employees' commitment to their organizations' values. Without commitment to the organization's values, pay-for-performance made employees *less likely* to do things that would help the organization's purposes but weren't measured as part of their duties. When employees were committed to the organization's values, however, pay-for-performance didn't discourage that extra effort. People performed above and beyond the call of duty because they cared, even if it wasn't extrinsically rewarded.

If you've agreed with the thinking of this book, then, you'll want to help build intrinsic motivation in work teams. This means making sure that as many as possible of the building blocks are there for creating a sense of *meaningfulness, choice, quality,* and *progress* in workers' jobs.

But pay is still important to most workers. This raises the question of how to treat it.

Treating Pay as an Equity Issue

On performance issues, I think of extrinsic motivation as something that supplements intrinsic motivation. In other words, extrinsic incentives can have a greater influence on behavior when intrinsic motivation is moderate to low. But if intrinsic motivation is already high—with people self-managing and highly energized—monetary incentives provide little or no additional force. Past some point, it simply becomes impossible to be "more motivated" in any sustainable way. So if you are successful in building high intrinsic motivation, don't expect your pay system to have a major positive effect on performance.

With pay systems, on the whole, the best you can hope for is perceived fairness—or equity—so that pay doesn't become a distractor. *Equity* is a principle of fairness that basically says that your outcomes (rewards) should be proportional to your inputs (performance). It comes into play in comparisons between people or groups, and only becomes a motivational force when it is violated. Equity is violated when workers see that others in comparable jobs are paid more for the same level of performance, or when they find that others are paid the same even though they are performing at lower levels. When that happens, pay issues take center stage for workers, and people want to remedy the situation. But when pay is seen as equitable, workers' attention can return to their work tasks.

What does it mean to treat pay as primarily an equity issue? It means making sure that pay reflects performance in a reasonable manner, so that workers see that they are treated fairly. It means trying to avoid perceived inequities and to fix those that do occur. It does not mean assuming that workers are doing good work primarily to get higher pay. Wanting fair "pay for performance" is not the same as "performing for the pay."

When you talk to workers about motivational issues, then, put the task in the foreground—where it belongs—and put pay in the background. Talk about the intrinsic rewards and the building blocks. Stressing pay incentives is likely to insult workers who are committed to the task purpose and will introduce an element of cynicism into the climate. As a practical matter, a pay-for-performance system will still provide backup extrinsic motivation for a worker who is not highly intrinsically motivated. But the last thing you want to do is to assume that all your workers are motivated extrinsically and to treat them in that way.

Notes

Chapter 1. The Shift from Compliance to Partnership

1. I owe this insight to my colleague, Susan Hocevar. This chapter draws on a historical overview of empowerment from a working paper: Kenneth W. Thomas, Susan P. Hocevar, and Gail Fann Thomas, "Operational, Tactical, and Strategic Meanings of Empowerment: Historical Analysis, Interview Findings, and an Integrative Language" (Monterey, CA: Naval Postgraduate School, December 1998).

2. See Richard E. Walton, "From Control to Commitment in the Workplace," *Harvard Business Review,* 63, no. 2 (1985): 77–84.

3. Richard E. Walton, "Contrasting Designs for Participative Systems," *Personnel Administration,* 30 (November- December 1967): 35–41.

4. Warren G. Bennis, "The Coming Death of Bureaucracy," *Think Magazine,* November-December 1966, pp. 30–35. For an update on this theme, see Gifford Pinchot and Elizabeth Pinchot, *The End of Bureaucracy and the Rise of the Intelligent Organization* (San Francisco: Berrett-Koehler, 1994).

5. Jeffrey Pfeffer, *Competitive Advantage Through People: Unleashing the Power of the Work Force* (Boston: Harvard Business School Press, 1992).

6. Quoted in Noel M. Tichy and Stratford Sherman, *Control Your Destiny or Someone Else Will: How Jack Welch Is Making General Electric the World's Most Competitive Corporation* (New York: Currency Doubleday, 1993), p. 251.

Chapter 2. Extrinsic Rewards Are No Longer Enough

1. The notion that extrinsic rewards would tend to drive out intrinsic motivation was championed by Edward Deci in such books as *Intrinsic Motivation*

(New York: Plenum Press, 1975). In the psychology literature, this notion was called the "overjustification effect," a term coined by M. R. Lepper, D. Greene, and R. E. Nisbett in "Undermining Children's Intrinsic Interest with Extrinsic Reward: A Test of the Overjustification Hypothesis," *Journal of Personality and Social Psychology,* 28, no. 1 (1973): 129–137. Two recent scholarly reviews of the literature have shown that this effect occurs only under relatively constrained circumstances: J. Cameron and W. D. Pierce, "Reinforcement, Reward, and Intrinsic Motivation: A Meta-Analysis," *Review of Educational Research,* 64, no. 3 (1994): 363–423, and U. J. Wiersma, "The Effects of Extrinsic Rewards in Intrinsic Motivation: A Meta-Analysis," *Journal of Occupational and Organizational Psychology,* 65 (1992): 101–114. In business settings, extrinsic rewards were often found to be correlated positively with workers' reported intrinsic motivation.

2. This research was reported in two technical reports written for the U.S. Army Reserve: Kenneth Thomas, "Leadership and Retention in TPU's: A Framework," Technical Report NPS-SM–95–006, Naval Postgraduate School, 1995, and Kenneth Thomas and Bob Barrios-Choplin, "Effective Leadership in TPU's: Findings from Interviews at Sixteen Units," Technical Report NPS-SM–96–002, Naval Postgraduate School, 1996.

3. For a recent classic book on this topic, see Denise Rousseau, *Psychological Contracts in Organizations: Understanding Written and Unwritten Agreements* (Thousand Oaks, CA: Sage, 1995). The implications of the newer psychological contract for workers is described in Cliff Hakim, *We Are All Self-Employed: The New Social Contract for Working in a Changed World* (San Francisco: Berrett-Koehler, 1994).

Chapter 3. Getting Beyond Rational-Economic Assumptions

1. Herbert A. Simon, "A Behavioral Model of Rational Choice," *Quarterly Journal of Economics,* 69 (1955): 99–118.

2. Expectancy theory was first popularized in the management literature by Victor H. Vroom, *Work and Motivation* (New York: Wiley, 1964). Many textbooks now use the more user-friendly version of the theory introduced by Edward E. Lawler III, *Motivation in Work Organizations* (Monterey, CA: Brooks/Cole, 1973). Expectancy theory essentially predicts the motivation to engage in a behavior on the basis of the perceived probability (expectancy) that the behavior will lead to a given outcome, multiplied by the perceived value (valence) of that outcome. It is an adaptation of the expected value calculations familiar to economics.

3. Abraham H. Maslow, *Motivation and Personality* (New York: Harper & Row, 1954). Edgar H. Schein, *Organizational Psychology* (Englewood Cliffs, NJ: Prentice-Hall, 1965).

4. Amatai Etzioni, *The Moral Dimension: Toward a New Economics* (New York: Free Press, 1988).

Chapter 4. Purposeful Work

1. Kenneth W. Thomas and Betty A. Velthouse, "Cognitive Elements of Empowerment: An Interpretive Model of Intrinsic Task Motivation," *Academy of Management Review*, 15, no. 4 (1990): 666–681.

2. I have found Jay Galbraith's thinking most helpful in understanding how and why organizations have needed to change structure to cope with increased uncertainties in their environment. My analysis draws heavily upon his concepts. His ideas were developed in Jay Galbraith, *Designing Complex Organizations* (Reading, MA: Addison-Wesley, 1973) and in a number of subsequent books, and are heavily cited in most management texts.

3. The notion of uncertainty absorption was developed in James G. March and Herbert A. Simon, *Organizations* (New York: Wiley, 1958). The idea of buffering the organization's technical core from environmental influences was described in James D. Thompson, *Organizations in Action* (New York: McGraw-Hill, 1967). Both works were seminal in the development of the organizational sciences.

4. Peter Block, *Stewardship: Choosing Service Over Self-Interest* (San Francisco: Berrett-Koehler, 1994).

5. Frederick W. Taylor, *The Principles of Scientific Management* (New York: Harper & Row, 1911).

6. The breakthrough book on the effect of technology on organization was Joan Woodward, *Industrial Organization: Theory and Practice* (London: Oxford University Press, 1965). Breakthrough books on the effects of environmental uncertainty were Tom Burns and George M. Stalker, *The Management of Innovation* (London: Tavistock, 1961), and Paul R. Lawrence and Jay W. Lorsch, *Organization and Environment* (Homewood, IL: Irwin, 1969).

7. Peter B. Vaill, *Managing as a Performing Art* (San Francisco: Jossey-Bass, 1989), pp. 2–3.

8. Richard J. Leider, *The Power of Purpose* (San Francisco: Berrett-Koehler, 1997), p. 137.

9. Joseph Campbell, *Hero with a Thousand Faces* (Princeton, NJ: Princeton University Press, 1989).

10. The Viennese psychiatrist Victor Frankl, who himself survived the Nazi death camps, wrote powerfully of the importance of purpose in sustaining life, founding an influential branch of psychiatry based on that principle. The story of his experience, which also contained his philosophy, was an international best-seller in the 1950s and 1960s: Victor E. Frankl, *Man's Search for Meaning: An Introduction to Logotherapy* (New York: Washington Square Press, 1963).

11. Albert Camus, *The Myth of Sisyphus and Other Essays* (New York: Random House, 1955).

12. Studs Terkel, *Working* (New York: Ballantine, 1985), p. xiii.

13. For a description of the changing workforce and its implications for organizations, see David Jamieson and Julie O'Mara, *Managing Workforce 2000* (San Francisco: Jossey-Bass, 1991).

14. The distinction between transactional and transformational leadership was developed in the management literature by Bernard M. Bass, *Leadership and Performance Beyond Expectations* (New York: Free Press, 1985), using concepts from James McGregor Burns.

15. James M. Burns, *Leadership* (New York: Harper & Row, 1978).

16. For example: Bass, *Leadership and Performance Beyond Expectations;* Warren Bennis and Burt Nanus, *Leaders: The Strategies for Taking Charge* (New York: Harper & Row, 1985); James Kouzes and Barry Posner, *The Leadership Challenge* (San Francisco: Jossey-Bass, 1987).

17. James C. Collins and Jerry I. Porras, *Built to Last: Successful Habits of Visionary Companies* (New York: HarperCollins, 1994).

18. Collins and Porras, *Built to Last;* A. De Geus, "Companies: What Are They?" *RSA Journal,* June 1995, pp. 26–35.

19. De Geus, "Companies: What Are They?" p. 29, cited in Lee G. Bolman and Terrence E. Deal, *Reframing Organizations,* 2nd ed. (San Francisco: Jossey-Bass, 1977), p. 342.

20. Block, *Stewardship,* p. 5.

Chapter 5. Self-Management in the Pursuit of Purpose

1. B. F. Skinner, *Science and Human Behavior* (New York: Free Press, 1953).

2. William F. Dowling, "Managers or Animal Trainers (Interview with Frederick Herzberg)," *Management Review,* 60 (1971).

3. For a thorough academic review of the state of motivation research, see Ruth Kanfer, "Motivation Theory and Industrial and Organizational Psychology," in *Handbook of Industrial and Organizational Psychology,* vol. 1, 2nd ed., edited by Marvin D. Dunnette and Leaetta M. Hough, pp. 75–170 (Palo Alto, CA: Consulting Psychologists Press, 1990).

4. A first version of this model appeared in a technical report prepared for the Eighth Quadrennial Review of Military Compensation: Kenneth W. Thomas and Erik Jansen, "Intrinsic Motivation in the Military: Models and Strategic Importance," Technical Report NPS-SM-96-001, Monterey, CA: Naval Postgraduate School, September 1996. It was then adapted for broader publication in Kenneth W. Thomas, Erik Jansen, and Walter G. Tymon Jr., "Navigating in the Realm of Theory: An Empowering View of Construct Development," *Research in Organizational Change and Development,* 10 (1997): 1–30.

5. Gordon R. Sullivan and Michael V. Harper, *Hope Is Not a Method: What Business Leaders Can Learn from America's Army* (New York: Random House, 1996).

6. John Dewey (1859–1952) was an influential American advocate of Pragmatism in education and philosophy, stressing the fundamental role of in-

telligence and learning in solving the practical problems people encoun-
tered. See, for example: John Dewey, *How We Think* (Boston: Heath, 1933).

7. Peter M. Senge, *The Fifth Discipline: The Art and Practice of the Learning Organization* (New York: Doubleday, 1990).

8. For a classic article on coaching, see Roger D. Evered and James C. Selman,
"Coaching and the Art of Management," *Organizational Dynamics,* 18, no. 2
(Autumn 1989): 16–32.

9. Jack Welch's ideas have been publicized in a number of books. See Noel M.
Tichy and Stratford Sherman, *Control Your Destiny or Someone Else Will: How
Jack Welch Is Making General Electric the World's Most Competitive Corporation*
(New York: Currency Doubleday, 1993). The idea of boundarylessness has
been elaborated in a recent book by several of the main consultants to G.E.:
Ron Ashkenas, Dave Ulrich, Todd Jick, and Steve Kerr, *The Boundaryless
Organization: Breaking the Chains of Organizational Structure* (San Francisco:
Jossey-Bass, 1995).

10. Peter Block, *Stewardship: Choosing Service Over Self-Interest* (San Francisco:
Berrett-Koehler, 1994), p. 30.

11. Kenneth W. Thomas, Susan P. Hocevar, and Gail Fann Thomas, "Operational, Tactical, and Strategic Meanings of Empowerment: Historical Analysis, Interview Findings, and an Integrative Language" (Monterey, CA: Naval
Postgraduate School, December 1998), p. 21.

Chapter 6. The Rewards of Self-Management

1. Stephen R. Covey, *The Seven Habits of Highly Effective People: Restoring the
Character Ethic* (New York: Simon & Schuster, 1989); Stephen R. Covey,
Principle-Centered Leadership (New York: Fireside, 1990).

2. This set of intrinsic rewards has evolved over time as my colleagues and I
have analyzed more data and refined our insights. Much of this evolution
is described in Kenneth W. Thomas, Erik Jansen, and Walter G. Tymon Jr.,
"Navigating in the Realm of Theory: An Empowering View of Construct
Development," *Research in Organizational Change and Development,* 10
(1997): 1–30. The first theoretical publication of the model, in Kenneth W.
Thomas and Betty A. Velthouse, "Cognitive Elements of Empowerment:
An Interpretive Model of Intrinsic Task Motivation," *Academy of Management Review,* 15, no. 4 (1990): 666–681, listed meaningfulness, choice, com-
petence, and impact. In later empirical and theoretical work with Walt
Tymon, it became clearer that what we had earlier referred to as "impact"
in the model was actually a sense of progress.

3. Kenneth W. Thomas and Walter G. Tymon Jr., *Empowerment Inventory* (Palo
Alto, CA: Consulting Psychologists Press, 1993). (The *Empowerment Inventory* was originally published by Xicom, in Tuxedo, New York, which was
acquired in 1999 by Consulting Psychologists Press.)

4. Thomas and Tymon, *Empowerment Inventory,* p. 9.

5. This figure is adapted from Figure 2 in Kenneth Thomas and Erik Jansen, "Intrinsic Motivation in the Military: Models and Strategic Importance," Technical Report NPS-SM–96–001, Monterey, CA: Naval Postgraduate School, September 1996, p. 16.

6. Research findings are briefly summarized in Kenneth W. Thomas and Walter G. Tymon Jr., "Bridging the Motivation Gap in Total Quality," *Quality Management Journal,* 4, no. 2 (1997): 80–96, and in Thomas et al., "Navigating in the Realm of Theory." For a couple of specific studies, see Kenneth W. Thomas and Walter G. Tymon Jr., "Does Empowerment Always Work: Understanding the Role of Intrinsic Motivation and Personal Interpretation," *Journal of Management Systems,* 6, no. 2 (1994): 1–13; Gretchen M. Spreitzer, "Psychological Empowerment in the Workplace: Dimensions, Measurement, and Validation," *Academy of Management Journal,* 38, no. 5 (1995): 1442–1465.

7. W. Edwards Deming used the term "intrinsic motivation" in W. Edwards Deming, *The New Economics for Industry, Government, Education* (Cambridge, MA: MIT Center for Advanced Engineering Study, 1993) and in his videotape series, W. Edwards Deming, *The Deming Library* (Chicago: Films Incorporated, 1991), especially Volume XV. He also used the term "joy in work" in *The New Economics.* He used the term "pride of workmanship" in his earlier book: W. Edwards Deming, *Out of the Crisis* (Cambridge, MA: MIT Center for Advanced Engineering Study, 1986).

8. Thomas and Tymon, *Empowerment Inventory.*

9. Thomas and Tymon, *Empowerment Inventory.*

10. J. Richard Hackman, Greg Oldham, Robert Janson, and Kenneth Purdy, "A New Strategy for Job Enrichment," *California Management Review,* 17, no. 4 (1975): 57–71; J. Richard Hackman and Greg R. Oldham, *Work Redesign* (Reading, MA: Addison-Wesley, 1980).

11. See the discussion of the role of interpretation in Thomas and Velthouse, "Cognitive Elements of Empowerment." That initial conceptual model identified individual differences in interpretive "styles" that were expected to influence intrinsic motivation. A later study by Thomas and Tymon, "Does Empowerment Always Work," identified a number of interpretive styles that influenced intrinsic motivation. Walt Tymon and I have continued to work with these interpretive styles and their effects, especially their contribution to stress. See Kenneth W. Thomas and Walter G. Tymon Jr., "Interpretive Styles That Contribute to Job-Related Stress: Two Studies of Managerial and Professional Employees," *Anxiety, Stress, and Coping,* 8 (1995): 235–250; as well as a training instrument based upon this research, Kenneth W. Thomas and Walter G. Tymon Jr., *Stress Resiliency Profile* (Palo Alto, CA: Consulting Psychologists Press, 1992). For a broad description of the role of managers' interpretive framing of events, see Lee G. Bolman

and Terrence E. Deal, *Reframing Organizations,* 2nd ed. (San Francisco: Jossey-Bass, 1977).

12. Again, such leaders frame the purpose in terms that appeal to people's underlying values and create compelling visions of what it would be like to achieve that purpose. These are creative acts of interpretation that help people construct new meanings for a task purpose.

13. Charles C. Manz, *Mastering Self-Leadership* (Englewood Cliffs, NJ: Prentice-Hall, 1992).

Chapter 7. Building a Sense of Meaningfulness

1. This notion of life stages and transitions has been familiar since the publication of two classic works in the 1970s: Daniel J. Levinson, *The Seasons of a Man's Life* (New York: Ballantine, 1979), and Gail Sheehy, *Passages: Predictable Crises of Adult Life* (New York: Dutton, 1976). See also the more recently published book by Daniel J. Levinson, *The Seasons of a Woman's Life* (New York: Ballantine, 1996).

2. For creative ways of enhancing this fit, see David Jamieson and Julie O'Mara, *Managing Workforce 2000* (San Francisco: Jossey-Bass, 1991).

3. There have been a number of recent management books that mention soul or spirit in the context of finding meaning in work. Here are a few: Peter Block, *Stewardship: Choosing Service Over Self-Interest* (San Francisco: Berrett-Koehler, 1994); Richard J. Leider, *The Power of Purpose* (San Francisco: Berrett-Koehler, 1997); Jack Hawley, *Reawakening the Spirit in Work* (San Francisco: Berrett-Koehler, 1993); Lee G. Bolman and Terrence E. Deal, *Leading with Soul* (San Francisco: Jossey-Bass, 1995); Keshavan Nair, *A Higher Standard of Leadership: Lessons from the Life of Gandhi* (San Francisco: Berrett-Koehler, 1994); and Alan Green, *A Company Discovers Its Soul* (San Francisco: Berrett-Koehler, 1996).

4. Frank Sinatra, vocalist, "That's Life," words and music by Dean Kay and Kelly Gordon, Reprise Records, 1966.

5. Block, *Stewardship,* pp. 221–231.

6. Block, *Stewardship,* p. 3.

7. This quote is from John Madden, *Hey, Wait a Minute* (New York: Ballantine-Fawcette, 1985) and was cited in James Kouzes and Barry Posner, *The Leadership Challenge* (San Francisco: Jossey-Bass, 1987), p. 89.

8. This is the title of chapter 5 in James C. Collins and Jerry I. Porras, *Built to Last: Successful Habits of Visionary Companies* (New York: HarperCollins, 1994).

9. Kouzes and Posner, *The Leadership Challenge,* p. 88.

10. Quoted in Noel Tichy and Ram Charan, "Speed, Simplicity, Self-Confidence: An Interview with Jack Welch," *Harvard Business Review,* 67, no. 5 (September–October 1989): 119.

11. Again, the G.E. Workout process has been widely described. See chapter 16 in Noel M. Tichy and Stratford Sherman, *Control Your Destiny or Someone Else Will: How Jack Welch Is Making General Electric the World's Most Competitive Corporation* (New York: Currency Doubleday, 1993).

12. J. Richard Hackman and Greg R. Oldham, *Work Redesign* (Reading, MA: Addison-Wesley, 1980), p. 78.

13. This line is from Act III of Oscar Wilde's play *Lady Windermere's Fan*.

14. Kenneth W. Thomas and Walter G. Tymon Jr., "Does Empowerment Always Work: Understanding the Role of Intrinsic Motivation and Personal Interpretation," *Journal of Management Systems*, 6, no. 2 (1994): 1–13.

15. Thomas and Tymon, "Does Empowerment Always Work;" Kenneth W. Thomas and Walter G. Tymon Jr., "Interpretive Styles That Contribute to Job-Related Stress: Two Studies of Managerial and Professional Employees," *Anxiety, Stress, and Coping*, 8 (1995): 235–250.

16. These recommendations are spelled out in greater detail in Kenneth W. Thomas and Walter G. Tymon Jr., *Stress Resiliency Profile* (Palo Alto, CA: Consulting Psychologists Press, 1992).

17. Leider, *The Power of Purpose*, p. 26.

18. Leider, *The Power of Purpose;* Cliff Hakim, *We Are All Self-Employed* (San Francisco: Berrett-Koehler, 1994); Richard Nelson Bolles, *What Color Is Your Parachute? A Practical Manual for Job-Hunters and Career Changers* (Berkeley, CA: Ten Speed Press, 1999).

19. Leider, *The Power of Purpose*, p. 70.

20. Peter Block, *The Empowered Manager* (San Francisco: Jossey-Bass, 1987), p. 102.

21. Leider, *The Power of Purpose*, pp. 67, 119.

22. Hackman and Oldham, *Work Redesign*, p. 78.

Chapter 8. Building a Sense of Choice

1. The three stages described here—dependence, counterdependence, and interdependence—are widely used now. They were introduced into the literature on organizational development by Warren G. Bennis and Herbert A. Shepard in "A Theory of Group Development," *Human Relations*, 9, no. 4 (1956): 415–437.

2. Chris Argyris, *Personality and Organization: The Conflict Between System and the Individual* (New York: Harper & Brothers, 1957).

3. This is a frequent theme in the literature on codependency. See, for example, John Bradshaw, *Bradshaw on: The Family* (Deerfield Beach, FL: Health Communications, 1988).

4. For example, this definition of self was prominent of the "est" movement introduced by Werner Erhard in the 1970s. For a somewhat sympathetic biography and statement of the est philosophy, see William W. Bartley III, *Werner Erhard* (New York: Potter, 1978). More recently this same notion

has been captured by viewing the self as "agent." See, for example, Barbara L. McCombs and R. J. Marzano, "Putting the Self in Self-Regulated Learning: The Self as Agent in Integrating Will and Skill," *Educational Psychologist,* 31 (1990): 819–833.

5. R. DeCharms, *Personal Causation: The Internal Affective Determinants of Behavior* (New York: Academic Press, 1968).

6. This link between autonomy (choice) and experienced responsibility for outcomes was described in J. Richard Hackman and Greg R. Oldham, *Work Redesign* (Reading, MA: Addison-Wesley, 1980), pp. 79, 80.

7. For example, see Victor H. Vroom and Phillip W. Yetton, *Leadership and Decision-Making* (Pittsburgh: University of Pittsburgh Press, 1973). This model of leadership styles as decision methods is included in most management texts.

8. Edward E. Lawler III, *From the Ground Up: Six Principles for Building the New Logic Corporation* (San Francisco: Jossey-Bass, 1996), p. 31.

9. Kenneth W. Thomas, Susan P. Hocevar, and Gail Fann Thomas, "Operational, Tactical, and Strategic Meanings of Empowerment: Historical Analysis, Interview Findings, and an Integrative Language" (Monterey, CA: Naval Postgraduate School, December 1998).

10. James C. Collins and Jerry I. Porras, *Built to Last: Successful Habits of Visionary Companies* (New York: HarperCollins, 1994), p. 152.

11. Steven Kerr, chief learning officer, G.E., personal communication.

12. David McNally, *Even Eagles Need a Push* (New York: Doubleday, 1991).

13. This is "Point 8" in W. Edwards Deming, *Out of the Crisis* (Cambridge, MA: MIT Center for Advanced Engineering Study, 1986).

14. Cited in Stuart Crainer, *The Ultimate Book of Business Quotations* (New York: AMACOM, 1998), p. 181.

15. See chapter I–8, "Support Fast Failures," in Tom Peters, *Thriving on Chaos: Handbook for a Management Revolution* (New York: Harper Perennial, 1988), pp. 314–324.

16. The quote is from chapter 6 of *Alice in Wonderland,* reprinted in Lewis G. Carroll, *The Annotated Alice* (New York: Wings Books, 1998), p. 88.

17. Ken Blanchard, John P. Carlos, and Alan Randolph, *Empowerment Takes More Than a Minute* (San Francisco: Berrett-Koehler, 1996), p. 34.

18. Steven Kerr, personal communication.

19. This is the title of a book on Jack Welch—Noel M. Tichy and Stratford Sherman's *Control Your Destiny or Someone Else Will: How Jack Welch Is Making General Electric the World's Most Competitive Corporation* (New York: Currency Doubleday, 1993).

20. Cliff Hakim, *We Are All Self-Employed* (San Francisco: Berrett-Koehler, 1994), p. 13.

21. Franklin Delano Roosevelt, First Inaugural Address, March 4, 1933.

22. Admiral William Rowley (then Captain Rowley), personal communication, February 1993.

23. Max DePree, *Leadership Is an Art* (New York: Doubleday, 1989), p. 65.
24. Lawler, *From the Ground Up*, p. 31.

Chapter 9. Building a Sense of Competence

1. Robert W. White, "Motivation Reconsidered: The Concept of Competence," *Psychological Review*, 66 (1959): 297–333.
2. Edward L. Deci, *Intrinsic Motivation* (New York: Plenum Press, 1975).
3. Dick Richards, *Artful Work: Awakening Joy, Meaning, and Commitment in the Workplace* (San Francisco: Berrett-Koehler, 1995).
4. Peter B. Vaill, *Managing as a Performing Art* (San Francisco: Jossey-Bass, 1989).
5. Mihaly Csikszentmihalyi, *Flow: The Psychology of Optimal Experience* (New York: Harper & Row, 1990).
6. W. Edwards Deming, *Out of the Crisis* (Cambridge, MA: MIT Center for Advanced Engineering Study, 1986).
7. Ashcroft is a British executive, cited in Stuart Crainer, *The Ultimate Book of Business Quotations* (New York: AMACOM, 1998), p. 221.
8. Deci, *Intrinsic Motivation;* Edward L. Deci and Richard M. Ryan, *Intrinsic Motivation and Self-Determination in Human Behavior* (New York: Plenum, 1985).
9. This term was coined by David L. Cooperrider. See Suresh Srivastva, David L. Cooperrider, and Associates, *Appreciative Management and Leadership: The Power of Positive Thought and Action in Organizations* (San Francisco: Jossey-Bass, 1990).
10. Terrence E. Deal and M. K. Key, *Corporate Celebration* (San Francisco: Berrett-Koehler, 1998), pp. 47–48.
11. Skill recognition was labeled an "interpretive style" and found to be related to sense of competence in Kenneth W. Thomas and Walter G. Tymon Jr., "Does Empowerment Always Work: Understanding the Role of Intrinsic Motivation and Personal Interpretation," *Journal of Management Systems*, 6, no. 2 (1994): 1–13. Low skill recognition was also found to predict stress in Kenneth W. Thomas and Walter G. Tymon Jr., "Interpretive Styles That Contribute to Job-Related Stress: Two Studies of Managerial and Professional Employees," *Anxiety, Stress, and Coping*, 8 (1995): 235–250. Our measure is included in Kenneth W. Thomas and Walter G. Tymon Jr., *Stress Resiliency Profile* (Palo Alto, CA: Consulting Psychologists Press, 1992).
12. Mihaly Csikszentmihalyi, *Finding Flow: The Psychology of Engagement in Everyday Life* (New York: Basic Books), pp. 29–30.
13. Csikszentmihalyi, *Finding Flow;* Csikszentmihalyi, *Flow.*
14. W. Edwards Deming, *The New Economics for Industry, Government, Education* (Cambridge MA: MIT Center for Advanced Engineering Study, 1993), p. 112.
15. James C. Collins and Jerry I. Porras, *Built to Last: Successful Habits of Visionary Companies* (New York: HarperCollins, 1994), pp. 115–121.

16. Scott is the British novelist, author of *Ivanhoe.* Cited in Crainer, *The Ultimate Book of Business Quotations,* p. 95.

17. Abraham Maslow, "The Need to Know and the Fear of Knowing," *Journal of General Psychology,* 68 (1963): 111–125.

18. Janelle Barlow and Claus Moller, *A Complaint Is a Gift: Using Customer Feedback as a Strategic Tool* (San Francisco: Berrett-Koehler, 1996).

19. Rick Nelson, "Garden Party," 1972, MCA Records.

20. Csikszentmihalyi, *Flow,* p. 210.

21. Cited in Crainer, *The Ultimate Book of Business Quotations,* p. 183.

22. From William Shakespeare, *Hamlet,* Act I, Scene III.

Chapter 10. Building a Sense of Progress

1. Tom Peters, *Thriving on Chaos: Handbook for a Management Revolution* (New York: Harper Perennial, 1988), p. 366.

2. This quote is from a video, *Speed, Simplicity, and Self-Confidence: Jack Welch Talks with Warren Bennis* (Schaumburg, IL: Video Publishing House, 1993).

3. Kenneth W. Thomas and Walter G. Tymon Jr., *Empowerment Inventory* (Palo Alto, CA: Consulting Psychologists Press, 1993).

4. Harry Levinson, "When Executives Burn Out," *Harvard Business Review,* 59, no. 3 (May–June 1981): 72–81.

5. The original version of this model appeared in Kenneth W. Thomas, "Conflict and Conflict Management," in *Handbook of Industrial and Organizational Psychology,* pp. 889–935, edited by Marvin D. Dunnette (Chicago: Rand McNally, 1976), which was written in 1971—five years before its publication. It was a refinement of ideas developed in Robert R. Blake and Jane S. Mouton, *The Managerial Grid* (Houston: Gulf, 1964). The model evolved with later theoretical developments. The version presented here is adapted from Kenneth W. Thomas and Ralph H. Kilmann, *Thomas-Kilmann Conflict Mode Instrument* (Palo Alto, CA: Consulting Psychologists Press, 1974; originally published by Xicom).

6. For a more detailed account of the Camp David accords, see Shibley Telhami, *Power and Leadership in International Bargaining: The Path to the Camp David Accords* (New York: Columbia University Press, 1990).

7. For a diagnostic instrument that measures individuals' conflict-handling modes, see Thomas and Kilmann, *Thomas-Kilmann Conflict Mode Instrument.* This model is also explained and dramatized in a training video, *Dealing with Conflict* (Carlsbad, CA: CRM Films, 1992). For a practical guide to win-win negotiating, see Roger Fisher and William Ury, *Getting to Yes: Negotiating Agreement Without Giving In* (Boston: Houghton Mifflin, 1981).

8. D. Campbell, "If I'm in Charge, Why Is Everyone Laughing?" Paper presented at the Center for Creative Leadership, Greensboro, N.C., 1983. Cited in Lee G. Bolman and Terrence E. Deal, *Reframing Organizations,* 2nd ed. (San Francisco: Jossey-Bass, 1977), p. 351.

9. Satchel (Leroy) Paige, from his 1953 book, *How to Keep Young.* Quoted in John Bartlett, *Familiar Quotations,* 15th ed. (Boston: Little, Brown, 1980), p. 867.

10. Terrence E. Deal and M. K. Key, *Corporate Celebration* (San Francisco: Berrett-Koehler, 1998).

11. Edward E. Lawler III, *From the Ground Up: Six Principles for Building the New Logic Corporation* (San Francisco: Jossey-Bass, 1996), p. 29.

12. Lawler, *From the Ground Up,* p. 29.

13. J. Richard Hackman and Greg R. Oldham, *Work Redesign* (Reading, MA: Addison-Wesley, 1980), pp. 137–138.

14. Peters, *Thriving on Chaos,* pp. 330, 582.

15. These are habits four through six in Stephen R. Covey, *The Seven Habits of Highly Effective People: Restoring the Character Ethic* (New York: Simon & Schuster, 1989)

16. This phrase was used in Dean G. Pruitt, "Strategic Choice in Negotiation," *American Behavioral Scientist,* 27 (1983): 167–194. See also Dean G. Pruitt and Jeffrey Z. Rubin, *Social Conflict: Escalation, Stalemate, and Settlement* (New York: Random House, 1986).

17. Deal and Key, *Corporate Celebration,* p. 116.

18. Peters, *Thriving on Chaos,* p. 366.

19. Bob Nelson, *One Thousand and One Ways to Energize Employees* (New York: Workman, 1997), p. 66.

20. Nelson, *One Thousand and One Ways to Energize Employees,* p. 65.

21. Cited in Nelson, *One Thousand and One Ways to Energize Employees,* p. 90.

Chapter 11. Implications

1. Cliff Hakim, *We Are All Self-Employed* (San Francisco: Berrett-Koehler, 1994), p. 115.

2. For information on 360-degree appraisals, see Richard Lepsinger and Antoinette D. Lucia, *The Art and Science of 360° Feedback* (San Francisco: Pfeiffer, 1997).

3. From General Electric's 1991 Annual Report. Also cited in Noel M. Tichy and Stratford Sherman, *Control Your Destiny or Someone Else Will: How Jack Welch Is Making General Electric the World's Most Competitive Corporation* (New York: Currency Doubleday, 1993), p. 230. For related statements by Welch, see Janet Lowe, *Jack Welch Speaks* (New York: Wiley, 1998), pp. 89–92.

4. These internal labor markets were recently described by Harvard Business School professor Gary Hamel in "Bringing Silicon Valley Inside," *Harvard Business Review,* 77, no. 5 (September- October 1999): 70–84.

5. The *Myers-Briggs Type Indicator,* developed by Isabel Briggs Myers and Katharine C. Briggs, is available in different forms from Consulting Psychologists Press, Palo Alto, CA. It is probably the most widely used personality instrument today.

6. For a more complete description of the personality dimensions and types measured by the *MBTI,* as well as their importance in organizations, see Sandra Krebs Hirsh and Jean M. Kimmerow, *Introduction to Type in Organizations,* 3rd ed. (Palo Alto, CA: Consulting Psychologists Press, 1998).

7. Michael B. McCaskey, *Framework for Analyzing Work Groups,* document 480-009 (Cambridge, MA: Harvard Business School, 1985), p. 10. This teaching note is still widely used to teach the systems approach at the level of a work group.

8. Dick Richards, *Artful Work: Awakening Joy, Meaning, and Commitment in the Workplace* (San Francisco: Berrett-Koehler, 1995), p. 113.

9. Beverly Kaye and Sharon Jordan-Evans, *Love 'Em or Lose 'Em: Getting Good People to Stay* (San Francisco: Berrett-Koehler, 1999). Beverly Kaye is also author of *Up Is Not the Only Way: A Guide to Developing Workforce Talent,* 2nd ed. (Palo Alto, CA: Consulting Psychologists Press, 1997).

10. Beverly Kaye, personal communication, Sept. 9, 1999.

11. Cliff Hakim, *We Are All Self-Employed,* p. 14.

Appendix A. Two Earlier Models of Intrinsic Motivation

1. This section is based largely on the more detailed discussions in Kenneth W. Thomas and Walter G. Tymon Jr., "Bridging the Motivation Gap in Total Quality," *Quality Management Journal,* 4, no. 2 (1997): 80–96, and in Kenneth W. Thomas, Erik Jansen, and Walter G. Tymon Jr., "Navigating in the Realm of Theory: An Empowering View of Construct Development," *Research in Organizational Change and Development,* 10 (1997): 1–30.

2. For a statement of the model and summary of initial research findings, see Edward L. Deci, *Intrinsic Motivation* (New York: Plenum Press, 1975).

3. Edward L. Deci and Richard M. Ryan, *Intrinsic Motivation and Self-Determination in Human Behavior* (New York: Plenum, 1985).

4. Edward L. Deci with Richard Flaste, *Why We Do What We Do* (New York: Grosset/Putnam, 1995).

5. Again, this has been called the "overjustification effect." Recent, more definitive studies of this issue have used meta-analysis techniques that combine the large number of individual studies that have been done on this issue and measure the significance of the effect for all the studies taken together. Two of these analyses have shown that the overjustification effect happens only under very constrained circumstances: J. Cameron and W. D. Pierce, "Reinforcement, Reward, and Intrinsic Motivation: A Meta-Analysis," *Review of Educational Research,* 64, no. 3 (1994): 363–423, and U. J. Wiersma, "The Effects of Extrinsic Rewards in Intrinsic Motivation: A Meta-Analysis," *Journal of Occupational and Organizational Psychology,* 65 (1992): 101–114. In organizational settings, extrinsic rewards tend to be positively related to reported intrinsic motivation.

6. J. Richard Hackman, Greg Oldham, Robert Janson, and Kenneth Purdy, "A New Strategy for Job Enrichment," *California Management Review,* 17, no. 4 (1975): 57–71; J. Richard Hackman and Greg R. Oldham, *Work Redesign* (Reading, MA: Addison-Wesley, 1980).

7. Herzberg's well-known model was published in Frederick Herzberg, Bernard Mausner, and Barbara Snyderman, *The Motivation to Work* (New York: Wiley, 1959). It lost credibility in the academic literature when empirical studies failed to support it. See Robert J. House and L. A. Wigdor, "Herzberg's Dual-Factor Theory of Job Satisfaction and Motivation: A Review of the Evidence and a Criticism," *Personnel Psychology,* 20, no. 4 (1967): 369–389. Also see E. A. Locke, "Personnel Attitudes and Motivation," *Annual Review of Psychology,* 26 (1975): 457–480.

8. See the relevant portions of these two reviews of research results on the Hackman-Oldham model: Y. Fried and G. R. Ferris, "The Validity of the Job Characteristics Model: A Review and Meta-Analysis," *Personnel Psychology,* 40, no. 2 (1987): 287–322; and R. W. Renn and R. J. Vandenberg, "The Critical Psychological States: An Underrepresented Component in Job Characteristics Model Research," *Journal of Management,* 21, no. 2 (1995): 279–303.

Appendix B. Putting Money in Perspective

1. John R. Deckop, Robert Mangel, and Carol C. Cirka, "Getting More Than You Pay For: Organizational Citizenship Behavior and Pay-for-Performance Plans," *Academy of Management Journal,* 42, no. 4 (1999): 420–428.

Index

Deficiency focusing, 59, 81, 87
Delayed gratification, logic of, 12
Deming, W. Edwards, 46, 68, 80, 83, 84
DePree, Max, 75
Development, worker, 35–36, 67
Dewey, John, 34
Diagnosis, effective, 108
Disney Corporation, 111
Diversity, in passions, 52–53
Dreams, 56

E

Efficiency work, 20
Egypt, 94, 95
Eisenhower, Dwight D., 68
Eldercare, 9
Emotions: charges of, in self-management, 42–43; and intrinsic rewards, 12–13; as utilities, 12–13
Employee, versus associate, 3
Empowerment, 3
Empowerment Inventory (Thomas and Tymon), 43, 44, 48, 93
Energy. *See* Commitment
Equity, 119–120
Ethical standards, 32
Etzioni, Amatai, 13
Even Eagles Need a Push (McNally), 68
Expectancy theory, 10
Extrinsic rewards: control of behavior through, 27; intrinsic rewards versus, 7–8; in motivation theory, 6–9; and top management, 6–9

F

FAA. *See* Federal Aviation Administration
Fear: management by, 46; not yielding to, 73–75
Federal Aviation Administration (FAA), 18
Feedback: appreciative, for sense of competence, 80–81, 87; and learning, in self-management, 34–35;

listening to, for sense of competence, 86–87
Feelings, importance of, 111
Flaste, Richard, 115
Flexplace, 9
Flextime, 9
Flow, 83
Framing of events, 49
Free agency, 8–9
Freedom of thought, 31
French Existentialist movement, 22

G

GE. *See* General Electric
General Electric (GE), 5, 35, 58, 67, 71, 93
Global competition, 4; and retention, 8–9
Global marketplace, 4, 21
Guaranteed employment, 8

H

Hackman, J. Richard, 48, 58, 62, 99, 116
Hakim, Cliff, 72, 108, 114
Hamlet (Shakespeare), 89
Handing-off, 47
Harper, Michael V., 30
Hero with a Thousand Faces, The (Campbell), 22
Herzberg, Frederick, 27, 116
Hierarchies: tall, 4, 6; and uncertainties, 21
Hocevar, Susan P., 36, 66–67
Hope Is Not a Method: What Business Leaders Can Learn from America's Army (Sullivan and Harper), 30
Human resources: as important source of competitive advantage, 5
Hygiene factors, Herzberg theory of, 116

I

Improvements: individual, 104–105; measuring, 99–100
Industrial era, 19–20

Security, providing, 68–69

Self-determination, in Deci model, 115–116

Self-management, 7; and choosing activities to accomplish the purpose, 30–31; and committing to meaningful purpose, 29–30; events of, 28–35; feedback and learning in, 34–35; and loss of managerial control, 35–36; monitoring for competence in, 31–32; monitoring for progress in, 32–33; process of, 28; in pursuit of purpose, 26–37; rewards of, 41–50; worker, 26–27; and worker development, 36–37

Self-reinforcing cycle, 45

Senge, Peter M., 34

Service, 25

Shakespeare, William, 88

Shell, 111

Silicon Valley, 23

Simon, Herbert A., 10

Sinatra, Frank, 54

Sisyphus, myth of, 22–23

Skill: recognition of, 80–81; recognition of own, 87–88

Skinner, B. F., 27

Sound management, 3

Speed, 100

Spiritual passion, 53

Spreitzer, Gretchen M., 46

Standards: fostering high, 83–85; internal, versus external, 32; setting high, for self, 88–90

Stanford University, 5

Stewardship (Block), 54

Subordinate, use of, 3

Sullivan, Gordon R., 30

Supervision, close, 7

T

Tall hierarchies, 4, 6

Task activities, and intrinsic rewards, 42–43. *See also* Tasks

Task purposes, 18–19, 24, 42–43, 57–58. *See also* Purposes

Tasks: elasticity of notion of, 113; monitoring for progress of, 33; negotiating whole, for self, 62; and provision of whole, 58; relevance of, 61–62; in work, 17–18

Taylor, Frederick Winslow, 20

Technological change, 4, 21

Terkel, Studs, 23

Thomas, Gail Fann, 36, 66–67

Thomas, Kenneth W., 28, 36, 43–46, 48, 82, 93–95

Thomas-Kilmann Conflict Mode Instrument (Thomas and Kilmann), 94, 95

Thought, freedom of, 31

3M, 67

Thriving On Chaos: Handbook for a Management Revolution (Peters), 69

Time and motion work, 20

Transactional leadership, 24

Transformational leadership, 24

Trust: demonstration of, 67–68; earning of, 72–73

Tymon, Walter G., Jr., 28, 43, 44, 46, 48, 59, 61, 82, 93

U

Uncertainties: and bureaucratic management, 21; increased control over, 35; and self-management, 31–32

United Nations, 95

United States Marine Corps, 83

University of California at Los Angeles (UCLA), 112

University of Illinois, 116

V

Vaill, Peter B., 21, 79

Velthouse, Betty A., 18, 46

Vision: crafting a personal, 60–61; providing, for meaningfulness, 56–57

About the Author

Ken Thomas has made a career of finding meaningful challenges that face people in organizations, studying them until he understands the basic issues involved, and then giving people new choices for dealing with them. He is probably best known for his work on conflict. He described behavioral choices in conflict situations in a simple, two-dimensional model that has given millions of people important new insights. The *Thomas-Kilmann Conflict Mode Instrument,* which he designed with Ralph Kilmann, has sold three million copies and is translated into several languages. His video for CRM Films, *Dealing with Conflict,* is also a top seller.

His work combines respected research with practical training and consulting. He has worked with a wide variety of organizations—from oil companies to various branches of the military. After his earlier work on conflict, he has developed training instruments on power, stress, and intrinsic motivation. Most recently, he has been doing applied research and consulting on leadership.

Academically, Ken has been a professor of management at UCLA, Temple University, and the University of Pittsburgh, where he was also director of the Ph.D. program. He is currently professor of management at the Naval Postgraduate School in Monterey, California. He holds a Ph.D. from Purdue University in administrative sciences. Although he has written a large number of journal articles, this is his first book.

Ken lives with his wife, Gail, and their young daughter, Sarah, in Monterey. He enjoys hiking along the Big Sur coastline.